Treasures
of the
ANCIENTS

Treasures
of the
ANCIENTS

Stephen B. Shaffer

ISBN: 1-55517-282-2

Published and Distributed by:

925 North Main, Springville, UT 84663 • 801/489-4084

CFI

Cedar Fort, Incorporated

CFI Distribution • CFI Books • Inside Cougar Report
Tapestry Press • Health & Wellness Report

Cover Design by Lyle Mortimer
Page Layout and Design by Corinne A. Bischoff
Printed in the United States of America

PREFACE

My first attempt to translate old rock writings and symbols took me into the realm of the Spanish miners and the known Indian tribes throughout the west. Like thousands of people before me I marveled at the sights I saw. Who were these ancient people? Where did they come from? Why did they all of a sudden disappear? More importantly, did they leave any records to tell of their existence? Why, when and who were these people—these people who worked the ground and built forts of rock and adobe? What about their writings?

One of the greatest enigmas of my study and the study of others like me is that so many of the discoveries of ancient writings have somehow found their way to the attention of scholars, only to be covered with doubt and distrust (as so many of the academics tend to disassociate themselves from the stigma of the unknown). I wonder sometimes if there is a supernatural purpose in the discovery of these writings and in the discovery of plates of various shapes and sizes. Why is it that there is never a complete and thorough investigation?

My thoughts remain in the knowledge that someday all these things will be open and seen by all that are worthy. The writings of the ancients and the translations of their words will come forth in due time. Will we be ready to receive them?

INTRODUCTION

In the Pearl of Great Price we are told writing was from the beginning and a genealogy was kept of the children of God.

And a book of remembrance was kept, in the which was recorded, in the language of Adam, for it given unto as many as called upon God to write by the spirit of inspiration; And by them their children were taught to read and write, having a language which was pure and undefiled.

The Lord said that two facts do exist, *"that there are two spirits, one being more intelligent than the other; there shall be another more intelligent than they; and that he (God) is more intelligent than them all."* Adam taught all of his children how to read and write, and that they used this tool is evident by the records that were kept. It is also evident that the pure language of Adam was polluted and continued to be so until the language was no more. But in the beginning God gave Adam a language that was pure, perfect and undefiled in every form. This Adamic language, now unknown, was far superior to any tongue which is now presently used. This first language spoken by man was either the celestial tongue of gods or such adaptation of it as was necessary to meet the limitations of mortality. God granted Adam and his posterity the gift to speak, read, and write this language.

From this we learn where language came from and how it was first given to Adam and Eve. It is true that we must first be believers and have faith in the creation. We must be believers in revelations and willing to believe the story of man's beginning on this earth, and with that faith we will know that God is the one who is at the head.

It is not known how long Adam remained in the Garden of Eden. I think we may safely conclude that he was there some time, and all the while he was in the presence of the Father, the Lord Omnipotent. From the Lord he received his early training and was not left to find his way blindly after having been given one or two commandments. The story says that the Lord spoke to Adam and gave him commandments. How could he give him commandments without speaking to him? What would be more natural than to believe that the Father would speak to him in his own language, and that the language used was perfect, for it was the language of celestial beings? We are informed that Adam and the Lord carried on conversations. How was this done unless Adam had been taught to speak? Therefore, all who have faith in the word of the Lord must know that Adam had a language; that his language was pure and perfect for it came from the Lord. All Latter-day Saints know this to be the case, for the Lord revealed to Moses, and later to Joseph Smith in the writings of Moses, that not only did Adam have the power of speech but he was taught also to read and to write, and records were kept by him and by his posterity.

Facsimiles #1, #2 and #3 from the Book of Abraham show what the Adamic language may have looked like. It may have been corrupted by the time these drawings were made, but all in all, they are as close to the real thing as one can get. The story of how the Prophet Joseph Smith acquired the Abraham Facsimiles is a very interesting one.

A Mr. Michael Chandler, of Dublin, had acquired several mummies that had been unearthed in Egypt. The reason behind Mr. Chandler receiving these mummies is not really known. After Mr. Chandler had the mummies, he moved to the United States where he took up the profession of antiquity dealer in the Philadelphia area. Mr. Chandler had not brought the mummies with him, but had them shipped to New York where he claimed them at the customs office in the spring of 1833. After he had paid the duties and freight costs, he took the mummies into his possession. It is strange that Mr. Chandler had not inspected the coffins when he first purchased the mummies. It was after he had received them in America that he opened the boxes to find that he had a couple of shrunken human cadavers. He was furious and was about to dismember the remains when he was stopped by a man on the street who apprised him of their value. Mr. Chandler was not to sure of the value of such a treasure, and it was for certain that he did not hold a romantic value for them.

Seeing a chance to make some money, Mr. Chandler began to display his cadavers at public exhibitions in an effort to recoup his loses at the customs house. Mr. Chandler had nine mummies that he exhibited in and around Philadelphia. He reported to the local newspaper that they were the "Nine Mummies of Thebes." It is not known for sure, but one report states that four of the mummies, one male and three females, ranged from 4 ft. 9 in. tall to 4 ft. 11 in. tall. Their ages ranged from about 25 to 60 years.

It was in late June of 1835 when Mr. Chandler made an appearance with four of his mummies in Kirkland, Ohio, having worked his way around the eastern part of the United States exhibiting the mummies and three or four rolls of papyrus covered with hieroglyphic figures. The papyri had been recovered by Mr. Chandler at the customs office in New York City when he unwrapped some of the mummies in an effort to satisfy the custom officials and himself as to the contents of the coffins.

Once in Kirtland, Mr. Chandler soon found out that there was a man who might shed some light on the hieroglyphic characters on the papyrus. This man, of course, was the Prophet Joseph Smith. A meeting was arranged and soon Mr. Chandler, Joseph Smith, Orson Pratt and a few others met to ascertain the authenticity of the hieroglyphs. Orson Pratt wrote of this meeting as reported:

> But it so happened that in traveling through the country, he (Chandler) visited Kirtland, Ohio, where the Prophet Joseph Smith resided, bringing the mummies and the ancient papyrus writings with him. Mr. Chandler had also obtained from learned men the best translation he could of some few characters, which however, was not a translation, but more in the shape of their ideas with regard to it, their acquaintance with the language not being sufficient to enable them to translate it literally. After some conversation with the Prophet Joseph, Mr. Chandler presented to him the ancient characters, asking him if he could translate them. The Prophet took them and retired to his room and inquired of the Lord concerning them. The Lord told him they were sacred records containing the inspired writing of Abraham when he was in Egypt, and also those of Joseph, while he was in Egypt; and that they had been deposited with these mummies, which had been exhumed. And he also inquired of the Lord concerning some few characters which Mr. Chandler, gave him by way of a test, to see if he could translate them. The Prophet Joseph translated these characters and returned them with the translation to Mr. Chandler; and who, in comparing it with the translation of the same few characters by learned men, that he had before obtained, found the two to agree. The Prophet Joseph having learned the value of these ancient writings was very anxious to obtain them, and expressed himself wishful to purchase them. But Mr. Chandler told him that he would not sell the writing, unless he could sell the mummies, for it would detract from the curiosity of his exhibition; Mr. Smith inquired of him the price which was a considerable sum, and finally purchased

the mummies and the writing, all of which he retained in his possession for many years.

Joseph Smith purchased the four mummies with the hieroglyphic inscriptions for $2,400. Those inscriptions have become a very important part of Mormon history. During the month of December 1835, Oliver Cowdery had just finished working on the hieroglyphics when he wrote a letter to William Frye of Gilead, Illinois:

This record is beautifully written on papyrus with black, and a small part, red ink or paint, in perfect preservation. The characters are such as you find upon the coffins of mummies, hieroglyphics, etc. With many characters or letters exactly like the present, (though probably not quite so square), form of the Hebrew without points. These records were obtained from one of the catacombs in Egypt, near the place where once stood the renowned city of Thebes, by the celebrated French traveler Antonio Lebolo (uncle to Mr. Michael Chandler); in the year 1831. He procured license from Mehemet Ali, then Viceroy of Egypt, under the protection of Chevalier Drovetti, the French Consul, in the year 1828; employed 433 men four months and two days, (if I understood correctly, Egyptian or Turkish soldiers), at from four to six cents per diem, each man; entered the catacombs June 7, 1831, and obtained eleven mummies. There were several hundred mummies in the same catacomb; about one hundred embalmed after the first order, and deposited and placed in niches, and two or three hundred after the second and third order, and laid upon the floor or bottom of the grand cavity, the two last orders of embalmed were so decayed that they could not be removed, and only eleven of the first, found in the niches. On his way from Alexandria to Paris he put in at Trieste, and after ten days illness, expired. This was in the year 1832. Previous to his decease, he made a will of the whole to Mr. Michael H. Chandler, then in Philadelphia, Pa., his nephew, whom he supposed to have been in Ireland. Accordingly the whole were sent to Dublin, addressed accordingly, and Mr. Chandler's friends ordered them sent to New York, where they were received at the Custom House, in the winter or spring of 1833. In April of the same year Mr. Chandler paid the duties upon his mummies, and took possession of the same.

Following the purchase of the mummies and papyri Joseph Smith exhibited them in the Kirtland Temple where many people of every description came to marvel at the curious antiquities. Some time later the mummies were given to the parents of Joseph Smith for safe keeping. Following the murder of Joseph at Carthage, Illinois, the mummies remained for several years in the possession of Lucy Mack Smith, who continued to exhibit them throughout Illinois. She charged a small fee for the privilege of seeing the mummies, and thus the few coins she made were used for her keep. Lucy Mack Smith died in 1855 and the mummies together with the papyri became the property of Emma Smith, the prophet's widow, who with the encouragement of her second husband, Major L. C. Didamon, sold them in 1856 to Mr. A. Combs. Mr. Combs did not hold on to the mummies very long. He immediately sold two of them, along with some of the papyri, to Edward Wyman, owner of Wyman's Hall, or museum in St. Louis. The mummies were on exhibit with the hieroglyphic writings at the museum. Soon the mummies were sold again, this time to Colonel John H. Wood. Two of the mummies found a final resting place at the Chicago Museum until Mrs. O'Leary's cow kicked the lantern over, which caused the great fire that destroyed most of the city of Chicago. It was supposed that the museum, papyri, and the mummies all disappeared in the raging fire. It is still unknown what happened to the rest of the mummies. It seems that they disappeared without a trace.

When Joseph Smith first acquired the record, he announced that the papyri contained the writings of Abraham and Joseph, both ancient biblical characters who had sojourned in Egypt. In 1842, he published for the first time several continuing articles in the *Times and Seasons*, the Nauvoo journal. The articles were his translations of the papyri and were titled the *Book of Abraham*. The new book became a part of the Mormon canonized scripture now known as the Pearl of Great Price. The promised translation of the writings of Joseph (who was sold into Egypt according to the Bible) were never published until the Prophet Joseph Smith began the business of translation, but then this was interrupted by the murder of the prophet.

The prophet Joseph, then, not only had the records of the Nephites and the Jaredites, but the records of father Abraham as well. Who were the Jaredites and where did they come from? An ancient American Jaredite prophet, by the name of Ether kept a record of the final destruction of his people between 600 and 300 BC. In the beginning of his book he tells about the Tower of Babel, and how the Lord was going to punish mankind by breeding the universal mother tongue into a variety of languages. The people pleaded with the brother of Jared to seek out the Lord and ask him to spare them, their families, and friends from this disaster. Their petitions were granted and they proceeded to migrate in a northerly direction, taking with them many different kinds of animals, including elephants, horses, cattle, fish in a special fish container made of animal skins. They took honeybees known to them as "Deseret." They took all manner of seeds, implements of every description, carts, clothing, and everything else that mattered. It is believed they finally reached the Caspian Sea where they camped for a while and then turned easterly and crossed the mountains into central Asia. They made boats and rafts to cross inland seas and soon they may have reached what we know as the coast of mainland China. It is believed that they made camp not too far from Mount Tai, China's holiest of her five holy mountains.

Jared was the leader of the group but the spiritual leader was his brother, Moriancumer. Ether describes him as "being a large and mighty man, and a man highly favored of the Lord." Whenever Jared needed divine inspiration, he would simply ask his brother to go and check it out with the Lord. It wasn't long before Jared asked his brother how they were going to cross the vast ocean which lay before them to reach the Land that God had promised them earlier.

Moriancumer inquired of the Lord and was shown in a vision a detailed diagram of a unique sailing craft which was capable of floating on top of the water, or submerged beneath the waves. Without a doubt these crafts were the world's very first submarines. With these windowless crafts it was apparent that light would be needed inside. But how was this to be accomplished? Needing to know the answer to this very important question, the brother of Jared took himself to an exceedingly high mountain, taking with him sixteen small transparent stones which he had made out of molten rock, and he did cry unto the Lord saying:

O Lord, thou hast said that we must be encompassed about by the floods. Now behold, O Lord, and do not be angry with thy servant because of his weakness before thee; for we know that thou art holy and dwellest in the heavens, and that we are unworthy before thee; because of the fall our natures have become evil continually; nevertheless, O Lord, thou hast given us a commandment that we must call upon thee, that from thee we may receive according to our desires.

Behold, O Lord, thou hast smitten us because of our iniquity, and hast driven us forth, and for these many years we have been in the wilderness; nevertheless, thou hast been merciful unto us. O Lord, look upon me in pity, and turn away thine anger from this thy people, and suffer not that they shall go forth across this raging deep in darkness; but behold these things which I have molten out of the rock.

And I know, O Lord, that thou hast all power, and can do whatsoever thou wilt for the benefit of man; therefore touch these stones, O Lord, with thy finger, and prepare them that they may shine forth in darkness; and they shall shine forth unto us in the vessels which we have prepared, that we may have light while we cross the sea.

As we read, we see that the Lord did indeed touch each one of the stones so there could be light in each of the vessels. In 1980, Dr. John Heinerman made a remarkable discovery while in China. Dr. Heinerman was in China with the American Medical Students Association. While there he received special permission from the Ministry of Archaeology to visit Taisan (the city located at the base of Mount Tai). It took two days of considerable red tape to grant him this since Taisan wasn't included in their group's original travel itinerary. His desire in going was to further investigate local legends which stated that the first Chinese emperor ascended Mount Tai many centuries ago to converse with the Chinese god. Upon his return he brought with him rocks that glowed in the dark, which were eventually placed in various temples throughout the land. From this story comes the historical reputation for the mountain's absolute holiness.

Dr. Heinerman discovered that much of the local folklore had disappeared as a result of Mao Tse-Tung's takeover of the country in 1949. However, enough fragments had survived in some of the older people to convince him that something of supernatural significance had taken place in ancient times with a religious leader. Several crucial parallels between the old legends and the account given by Ether strongly suggested to Heinerman that this was the mountain to which the brother of Jared went for his special needs. Dr. Heinerman claims that there was one woman who stayed behind when the Jaredites made their way across the ocean, and that this woman is the mother of the proto-Mongoloid people and the Hmong of Laos.

The questions asked by some people are, *"Were there people here on the American soil before the Jaredites?" "Is there evidence that there were people here after the demise of the Nephites?"* The answer to both questions is yes, and the evidence continues to mount. The intent of this author is to show the reader the close relationship between the Adamic language, Nephite language, Jaredite language and several other ancient languages of people that populated the North and South American continent before the

Jaredites and after the Nephites (but before Columbus). The evidence shown in this book will allow readers to judge for themselves as to the validity of the claims, to draw their own conclusions, and to study the facts.

A FACSIMILE FROM THE BOOK OF ABRAHAM
No. 2

CHAPTER 1
THE SANPETE MUMMY CAVE

The first time that I heard of the mummy cave of Sanpete County, Utah, was from my parents in the late 1950s. My father told me of a man by the name of John Brewer who came to him with evidence of a people who inhabited the mountains of central Utah hundreds of years ago. My father and mother were shown many artifacts made from copper, lead, and gold. They were also shown heavy stone boxes and many other things that were very interesting to see. Mr. Brewer wanted my father to help him investigate the findings that he made. My father at the time was very busy with a large family and couldn't help at that time. The following, however, are excerpts from Mr. John Brewer's personal journal:

MARCH 30, 1955

Went to work for Mr. Jack Shand, in Manti. While out in the field he came and ask me to go to the Keller Ranch to get some equipment. I met a Mr. George Keller and we got to talking about the fair. I mentioned that I was going to try and set up an arrowhead collection to put on display. He then told me about a cave back of the temple hill. He told me there were lots of arrowheads there.

MAY 10

I went and looked for the place but I couldn't find it so I went and ask[ed] him again where it was but all that I could get was a laugh from him. I thought that he was pulling a fast one on me so I let it go at that. I told Jack about it and he said to offer him some wine and I might get him to tell me then.

MAY 19

I went out to the Keller place and offered him some wine with the promise that he would show me the place he had told me about a while

1

back. He said that he would not only show me the place but he would show me the spot himself if I would get him another bottle. I got the bottle and he showed me the place. No wonder I couldn't find it, I was on the wrong hill. It wasn't on the temple hill at all but the one in back of it. I went into the cave and found 30 arrowheads right off. I went back to the truck and thanked the old man. I then ask how he came to know of the cave and he said that he and an Indian boy played there as an old hideaway. He said he had a lot of fun there.

MAY 27

Went to the cave and moved a little dirt and found a large piece of pine gum. I looked at it for a second and threw it to one side thinking I would chew on it once in a while when I worked in the cave. I found 15 arrowheads and a few pieces of pottery. One item that I don't and can't understand was a small rock about 6" by 4" by 1". It had been scraped and some kind of marks were on it. I thought that I had better cover the entrance of the cave so that no one would find it so I covered it and left.

MAY 29

I got a book on how to dig for things because I find that I like to do this kind of work just for fun. I then got the tools that I needed, a small brush, 1/4 inch screen plus a small shovel and a small pick and two large spoons. I went to the cave and did a little digging. At 2 feet 8 inches I found another thing that looks like a small book. It was covered with some kind of mud like pottery only not as hard. The mud like stuff is very hard to get off the metal. The book-like object is 2½ by 3½ by 4 inches. The metal is lead I think but I'm not sure. The pages that I looked at were marked with the same kind of marks as the rock that I found but they are a little more legible. I can see a scorpion like mark on the first page. The marks are not cut in but look like they are stamped in with some kind of tool but I can't be sure. I find that I don't know too much of what I am doing so I had better do a little more studying and see what I can come up with.

JUNE 10

I went back to the cave but I couldn't find it. I had hidden it too good. When I find it again I'll mark it so that I can always find it. (I searched for the rest of June and into the middle of September.)

SEPTEMBER 17

I found the cave again and marked it so that I wouldn't lose it again. I put a small green bottle on an old tree stump that was near the entrance. I went in the cave and did a little digging but didn't find anything. I took the piece of pine gum and cut a little off and threw it to the side and went on digging. With no luck I went home.

OCTOBER 5

I went to the cave because I read that sometimes there has been insects in pine gum so I found the chunk of pine gum and I looked it over but I couldn't see anything so I put it to the side. I'll cut it open some time and see if there is any on the inside when I come again. I looked for a while and found a few arrowheads but it got dark so I covered the cave and went home.

OCTOBER 6

I was at work and I got to thinking about Joseph Smith and I wondered if maybe this was anything like he went through but I don't think so because he was a better man than I am. But the thought wouldn't leave me all that day. When I got done with work I sat down and I thought about what had happened to Joseph Smith. Then I thought of the Book of Mormon and I went and got me one. I had read it many times but not like I was going to read it this time. If you have any doubts about anything ask of the Lord and it will be made known to you. I read that at the first of the book so I decided to try it and see. I then went to the cave and I ask but I never got the answer that I thought that I would and it took more than one time of asking the Lord in which I did.

OCTOBER 10

I read the Book of Mormon through but I didn't get as far with it as I thought for it was pretty hard to understand so I am going to read it much slower. I then went to the cave and was thinking how would the Lord let anyone know to do his will. Just how do you ask him for the help that you want. So again I ask[ed] for the help that I didn't understand and I needed some expert advice but not from man for all they would do is take it away from me and I didn't want that. Many things went through my mind. As I was digging I found another piece of a plate and I didn't feel too good about this because it was on a piece of metal that to men is very highly prized. It also has the same kind of markings on it. I put the cave as the base of the people or person that made these things so there must be a lot more here so if I dig it all out I might find out what I have here. This is where it came to me if you want something you must first look for it and then you must work for it and then make up in your own mind if it is right or not. So this is how the Lord is going to work it. I then took the piece of pine gum home with me and I am going to cut it open and see if I can find any insects inside of it.

OCTOBER 15

I was at home today and I took the pine gum and I cut a corner off but I didn't find any bug's but there was a piece of some kind of bark or wood. I then went to the cave and cut deeper into the pine gum and I found another piece of rock inside of it but this piece didn't have the same kind of marks. There weren't many marks on it but there were a few lines. I think that it is a map of some kind, that's all it could be but of what and where. Another thing to solve but how does a man find out these things. Ask of the Lord? He helped me get this far so he will help me get the rest of the way. What a find. It might lead to a gold mine or something much better. This day has been a very good day. The Lord has been good to me today.

OCTOBER 29

Went to the cave and looked at all that I had found. Now what should I do with it? Some of this stuff is worth a lot of money and I could be real rich but is that what I want. I thought this over very clearly and I decided to ask of the Lord and see what he says.

OCTOBER 30

I ask the Lord what to do but I have got no answer as yet so I must ask again and see if I don't receive an answer. I dug a little bit and decided to get some small bottles and put the soil into them so that I would or might be able to tell the age of some of the things that I dig out. I should have done this sooner. I looked at the map and I couldn't find anything on it that I knew, not even a sign. I seemed to know the place but I just couldn't place it. What to do. How does a person find out how to find a place on the earth with a map that he has but he doesn't know where it goes on the earth or what part, ye gods. I may have to take the whole earth and cut it down but I ought to just take Utah first and cut it into sections. But how does the map go. I don't have any directions—no north or south. I thought on this for some time when it came to me, I'll just move it all ways until I come up with the right way. Now it came to me—so this is the way that God is getting to me. Now I know that there is a God above. Now I knew that the Lord was going to work with me. What must I do to see that the things that I had went for His purpose and not mine. I am going to ask if Joseph Smith was truly one of his chosen and see if it is from the Lord or not for it could be from the other person. So if God makes it known to me that Joseph Smith was a true Prophet of God then I'll know that I have something that is his and not mine. This I know may take a little time so I must be patient and be very sure. I feel that it is but I can't go on just my feelings. I then went and did some more digging. I didn't find anything but I moved very slow for the way that I am digging now takes a lot of time for I am not digging like I did before.

NOVEMBER 3

I looked things over and I thought that I had better put the map so that I wouldn't lose it. I had a lot of loose dirt so I had better put it some place out of the way so I took it out and scattered it among the oaks. That way no one would see it and find the cave.

NOVEMBER 8

I thought of a way to find out if the map that I had went to Utah or not. I'll get a map of Utah and cut it into sections and take the map and see if I can match it up with anything in each section. It is going to take a lot of tiresome work but it is the only way that comes to my mind at the present. I got a large map of Utah and made a square about the size that I thought that the map might be in comparison with the earth. I made the map into a cut-up mess. I had 369 squares to cover. That's a lot of work and it sure is going to take a lot of time but I might enjoy it. I made a little bench at the cleared end of the cave and put both maps on it and started to see if my idea would work. I would start at the north end of the map and work to the south. What a mess. I sure couldn't find anything on the first two sections. This is going to take more time than I thought. Time I have a lot of and I do enjoy most of what I am doing. I cannot explain how I feel about how God works with me but I know that he is for I am not a very smart person and some of these things that come to me are not mine for I have not had any experience of this kind before so I can say that it could only come from God.

NOVEMBER 17

While reading the Book of Mormon I read that the Jaredites and the Nephites both came to the north but I don't think that it was the Nephites for their writing was very large. I found some on a cliff in back of the temple and it doesn't look like what I have here so I might can say that it was not the Nephites. I'll ask God and see. I did a little digging but I found nothing. I took the map and studied a section but drew a blank.

NOVEMBER 28

I went to study the map again to see if I could find anything out today. I went through a part but I got real tired so I did a little digging but I found only some small bones and a few pieces of pottery. The bones must be of a rat or rabbit—this I don't know. Looked at the small book but it didn't make anything come to light. I must ask God and see what to do. I haven't got an answer to my questions that I have ask[ed] before so what must I do? God must not have got what I asked before or I must not have ask[ed] the right way so I'll keep on trying. I looked over the other plate that I had to see if they were any different but they all looked the same to me. If I got some old Greek or Hebrew maybe I might come up with something. I found only one good arrowhead and that was all.

NOVEMBER 30

I was talking to Mr. J. A., and he told me that there was an Indian burial ground down west of Manti at his ranch so I went down and found it but I took nothing. They were put there to rest so I left them there. What did the Indians do for a living here and how many were here. The arrows that I have found don't show that they were a war-like people. I wonder if the people that lived in the cave were Indians, but I can't believe that they knew how to make any writing but I could be wrong, maybe they did. I'll ask God and see. I bet that the Lord gets tired of me asking and not doing much to find these things out for myself. I did find that people did live at the time that the Book of Mormon says so that much is right. I can't see any man or two men making a book like the Book of Mormon for the fun of it. It would take a man a long time to do that and you could find a lot wrong with it. The only way that it could be is that God was with Joseph Smith. That is the only way it could have happened so it must be true but I am still not sure.

DECEMBER 4

A stormy day today so I went to the cave. I looked at the map but all that I did was get very tired and came up with nothing. Even the digging that I did gave me nothing. A bad day all around. The next time I get free I'll go down west and see what I come up with. I covered the cave entrance and left for I wouldn't come back for a little while.

DECEMBER 9

I went down west to see if I could find anything. I went a long way into the hills and looked at a lot of holes but I found nothing. I did find a metal like ore but it wouldn't be worth mining. Not enough and there was no big vein to even look at. I was on my way home when I came to a small cut in a rock. I dug the entrance a little bigger and went inside. I could stand so I dug a little and I found an old helmet. It was old and I didn't know how to handle it so I dug all around it. I put my shovel blade under it and took my brush and took some of the dirt off. I saw that it was of a Spanish type. With that I left for it was dark and I don't like to walk in these hills after dark. I'll come back tomorrow.

DECEMBER 10

Went back over west and to the hole in the rock to move the helmet. I took some glass that came out of a car. I put the helmet on it and took it to the car and hid it in the back seat and went back to the hole. I dug some more and found the rest of the armor. I did the same with it. It was of a Spanish make. That says that they were here. The depth that I found them was first the helmet 2 ft. 4 ½ in. down and the armor was 4 ft. 2 in. down. It was dark and I called it a day.

DECEMBER 20

Went back over west to the hole and dug and I found a bag that was eaten almost up but the bottom was still in one piece. At the bottom was a spoon-full of gold dust. The rest had mixed with the dust and dirt. I tried to see if I could find any but after a while I knew that it was no use so I gave it up. I wonder what the armor was doing here—why wasn't there any bones here? I can't see a man leaving this behind—another mystery. I dug some more but I found only the floor of the hole and that was all. The place isn't very big so I cleaned it out but I found nothing more. I'll come again and see if I overlooked anything.[2]

JANUARY 6, 1956

I started to go to church to see if that would give me any help but I find that it doesn't help much because they only go through the same thing. I can see the Sacrament but the classes don't cover what I seek. I want to know of the people and how they lived so that I can find out and see if that is the way that it was but they don't teach that and I think that would be a good thing for we all would like that. I ask around and I found out that there were very few people that could give me what I wanted so I looked for some books and I found very few on what I wanted. I wanted to find out how far that the Jaredites and the Nephites had come to the north and all that I could find was they were back east where Joseph Smith found the plates. But which way did they go? If I could find that out I might put together what I have and the puzzle would fit but all I find is a blank wall. No one seems to know and no one will say what he thinks. Most everyone tells me to write to the church and they could tell me. I've written, now to wait and see.

JANUARY 14

Went to the cave and I prayed very hard but I never got an answer so I thought maybe I am on the wrong side for I haven't gotten an answer from anyone. So I ask God out right and to the point and I still didn't get an answer so I sat down and I thought. I might have to do more working and less asking. Then it came to me, ask for the wisdom to learn and understand what you have and how to put it to use. I have been asking for the wrong things and in the wrong way. For deep down in my heart I have been looking for riches and the glory of men. Now I know why God left me. I was on my own and I had forgotten Him and His purpose. For it is written that God's things are free and man's things must cost. So I then ask God to forgive me for it was I who was wrong not him for he knew me and what I wanted and was seeking. I got the best feeling that I have ever had so I knew that God had forgiven me. I went to the map and went over it but I covered only a few sections and I was very tired. But it had been the best day yet thanks to God.

JANUARY 18

I read the Book of Mormon slowly and I found that you must go through it bit by bit and the understanding will come. I can see now that the language has changed from when the book was written and reading it now. I must look at it in a different way by trying to put the people and the way that they lived and then the book was easy to read plus easy to understand. But who was the one that left the things that I have found and why didn't it make sense? It is very hard to put into place. I tried to find some old Greek and Hebrew in which I did but I couldn't put them together. I ran into a lot of problems like how does it fit and which way do I put the plate for if I turn it one way I can find some Greek and if I turn it another I find Hebrew and another I find nothing. If I read the Greek it doesn't make any sense and if I put the Hebrew to use I get nothing. It is like the map, I find nothing but I'll keep on trying and some day I might find something. My mind gets to feeling like a big blank. I might have to get someone to help me but who do I trust? I still haven't gotten any word from the church but I may have to wait a little longer.

JANUARY 27

Went to the cave and did some more with the map but still drew a blank. So I did a little digging and I found a big rock that had some things on it, not marks like the marks on the plate but funny ones. I like this find for I could find all kinds of things on it. I enjoyed making things out of the things that were on it. I could make men and dogs and other things like that but I don't think that was what was on it. The size of the rock is 8 inches high and 8 inches wide and 28 inches long. It is sanded and made as the other rocks that I have found. It was down to the floor of the cave 6 feet down and the dirt or dust is all just about the same color. There isn't too much to put into a bottle but I'll do it any way. This find sure makes me feel a lot better. But still the same question stays with me. Who did this and what is the purpose of it? Someday the answer will come to me if I keep working at it.

FEBRUARY 3

I showed some of the guys some of the things that I had and all that they did was laugh at me and say that I sure did a good job at making them. But they all wanted to know where I found them. I wouldn't tell them and they really made a joke out of it but I don't care because they don't understand it either so what else is new. So I took them home and I took the rest to the cave and I looked at all that I had and I knew that no one was going to believe me so I'll keep on like I always have. I'll dig my own answers up and then I'll know but I won't tell anyone again about these things, that I'll swear to. I dug a little but found nothing so I studied the map but it got me no where. I sat down and dug a little more and I found a bell-like thing made out of lead. It also had small marks on it so I put it with the others. It was down about (this is a guess for I forgot my tape so I couldn't get a good measure of the depth) 4 feet 9 inches. I'll mark it on the dirt and bring my tape and get it right.

FEBRUARY 12

Went to the cave and I found that I was off only one-half of an inch so I got a good guess on it. God sent me a book today and it helped me get a better idea on how the Book of Mormon people lived so it makes the book a lot more interesting. Why do I do this is still a mystery to me for I am not a person of learning. I think that God is pushing me a little for I am getting so I can't sleep at night. My wife even gets mad at me for staying up at night reading and trying to make some of the pieces fit together. But how else am I to find it out if I don't study about the thing that is bugging me? I try and tell her but she doesn't understand me at all but maybe some day she might. I then studied the map again but I drew a blank. I also did a little digging and found a small metal item that I can't put into place. At first I took it to be a small chisel but when I hit it I could see that it wasn't for it was too soft so I marked it "X"and put it with some of the other things. Today was a good day for God was with me.

FEBRUARY 23

I went to the cave today and sat looking out at the countrysides and I did a little thinking about the Book of Mormon. I tried to put into my mind Moroni coming to the temple hill and saying that a temple would someday be placed here. I wonder what the people thought that were watching. I also wonder if he was moving away from his enemies or if he was going through and telling the people to repent of their ways and come back to God. I think sometimes that I would like to have been there but if I was I would have went with the people that were there so I guess that I am glad that I wasn't. I wish that I knew all the answers to all of this but all that I can do is dig and look and study. If I keep it up I might get all the answers that I want. I have still gotten no answer from the church, but I guess that they get a lot of that kind of mail so I guess that I don't blame them. I know that we have a lot of people that would like to make a joke out of the L.D.S. people. But the more that I find the more I know how the prophet must have felt but I am going through very little of what he went through. I wish that I could have been as good as he must have been for he had the best teachers that anyone could have had. Now what do I have here? It just doesn't seem to fit into the Book of Mormon any place so what do I have? The only thing that I can put it with is the Jaredite people but did they come up this far or not. The writing that they did was very fine but did they make this and if they did, why don't they have a city, and if they did, where is it? (I did a lot of thinking along this line so I will not print much of it for some of it may sound a little funny to people and some of it is very personal to me and it may give something for people to laugh at, but if you want all that is my record, I'll get it to you but it will take a lot of time for it goes back eighteen years and a lot is repetition of the same thing).

FEBRUARY 25

Did a little study with the map today and I drew a blank. Doing that is about the hardest work that I have ever done and it is the most unrewarding for I am getting no place fast but what can I do about it for I still haven't found any better way of doing it. I was to church and I still think that they ought to have a class on the ancient people of the Book of Mormon—the way they lived, what they looked like and the things that they did. I am sure it would mean a lot to people. They could understand the Book of Mormon better. I know that they did keep a lot of records and they hid a lot for it to come out when and if God wanted them to. For a people to just build and then leave the places is not the answer and it seems that war is the only answer for they did war a lot so I think that there was a few people that didn't like war so they would leave and seek a safe place to live so it could be possible for them to be up this far. But did they have someone that knew how to write and if they did, wouldn't they take the writings with them? As I look at the map I seem to see the place but I cannot place it for it leaves me. It is like trying to remember a name and for the life of you it just doesn't come to you. Maybe the marks on the map are cities which are long gone with the earth—it makes me wonder. I changed and dug a little but I only got a few pieces of pottery. Another good day.

MARCH 2

I did a little more work on the map but I couldn't find anything so I dug a while. This didn't bring anything. I asked God again for the things that I wanted to know. I wonder what someone would do if he caught me calling on God like this. I bet they wouldn't let me forget it. But in a way I wouldn't mind for it might make them think twice and look for God. But they probably wouldn't claim Christ so I guess that they wouldn't look for God on their own. But if they did, think of the challenge that would be in front of them. But they would have to give up some of their drinking and playing around. They make fun of me that I don't go on some of their parties and play poker with them but I work to hard for my money to do that with it. I wonder what they would do in my place. I guess that they would sell most of it and have a good time on the money. But God says to put up treasures in heaven and not on the earth. This I do believe and I hope that I can put up just a little bit so that some of the things that I have done will not seem too bad in God's eyes. I guess I had better go home.

MARCH 9

Read some more of the Book of Mormon and I am beginning to see what a job it would have been to write a book like this one without the help of God. I wonder if God would give something like this to just anyone for I don't think that I am that good of a person to be in trust of stuff like this. I don't know that much of God either but I know that he is helping me in his own way. I shouldn't get so tired of doing what I am so I still can't see why I can't sleep nor seem to stay away from the cave for if I don't come up and dig I feel like I am going to blow up. Something deeps pushing me to seek out this thing that I am doing so I think that it is God that is doing it. I dug some today and I found some small bones but I think that it is something that the rats are bringing in here. If I found some bigger ones then it might be different but nothing like that has come out so I'll just put these with the others that I have found. You never know when I might find out something from them. At the floor level I found another bell-like object. This one has some more little marks on it but I don't know what they mean. I don't understand why they made them out of lead for the metal is soft and it doesn't hold its shape very well. But here it is. I wonder what the marks are and what they have to do with the other things. I am getting a little frightened of this stuff for each piece that I get just makes me that much more confused and I can't put it together. Sometimes I feel that a person was a little gone and did this to get at someone—that could be. I must not put it aside for I know a few guys that would do that to me if they could. I will have to look into it and make good and sure that I am not being played as the blunt-end of a joke. That I couldn't take. But then, on the other hand, they sure went to a lot of trouble to make a joke and I don't think that anyone would go to all of this trouble to do this. Plus if I don't get the map read in a reasonable time then I know that it will be a joke. I can base it on that. I have got to ask of God for some kind of way that I will be able to tell if it was. Only he can tell me that. Wow! It is past midnight. I had better go home.

MARCH 19

I studied the map. I thought that I had at last found the answer—we shall soon see. Then it came to me how will I find the place on the map to the place on the earth. Another problem to face. Just how will I do that. I went through all that I knew and nothing came to me. So I did a little more digging and found nothing. The new problem came up and I can't seem to see any answer. Why is it that when a man gets one thing solved another one comes up? I should have looked more into this before I started. A man gets the job of thinking that he has gotten one problem solved and another one takes its place. Now I know what thought brings—a man must take all the problems at once into consideration before he makes a move. Now I see why it takes much time before a smart man goes on a long trip. He thinks before he moves no matter how long it takes. I'll call on God and see.

MARCH 23

I did a lot of thinking and I decided to go over the map a few more times to make sure that I have the right place. I went over it and over it and it looked like I had the right place all right. But I'll go over it again to be sure. If it is I will know the north and south of the map. I'll know that much and I will have gotten the place located on a new map that I can read. So I guess that I have come out all right in the long run anyway. I went over the map again and I found that it didn't seem to fit so I'll go over it again and see if that will show me that I am right or wrong. It is getting late but I can't leave until I get through with the map. I took the map and turned it all ways. It looks like I have found the place all right but it sure is a long way from here. I'll have to buy me a new car or some kind of outfit to get there. Well, I guess that it is going to be a long time before I can get to the spot but I will have to try. Now back to the new problem at hand and see how I can solve that. Dug a little but I found nothing but three small arrowheads and a small Indian drill. My arrowhead collection is getting pretty large. I still wonder why they used such small ones. The game that they got with them must have been small to[o]. I also looked at some of the plates that I have and what I wouldn't give to know what they said. But I just don't have that kind of training. Just how this is done must come from a plate that has the other known language and it is put in comparison with the unknown one. It has got to be worked that way. I don't see any other way. It is 3 0'clock in the morning. I had better get home or my wife may get mad.

MARCH 28

I wonder if I'll ever get the answer to the way to locate the spot on the earth. I have looked and ask[ed] but everyone has a different way to do it plus they all cost too darn much. There has to be a cheaper way to do it. I did a lot of digging but I came up with nothing. My mind wasn't really on the digging so I'll just look at the items that I have and see if I get anything out of it. I looked at the one gold plate that I found and I cleaned it off with the brush and I compared it with the others and they all had the same kind of writing on them. I still can't see what the purpose was at leaving all of this stuff in this place. If the people left they would have taken all of this with them. But on the other hand, the person that made them might still be here so I might find some bones of a human being here so I must be careful with my digging. This gives me something to think upon any way.

MARCH 30

I found a way to locate a spot on the earth at last. It came to me one night as I was laying in bed. I was thinking of some of the guys that were in the army with me and what they were doing now and I thought of the compass course that we went through to pass it. That's when it came to me. I had the answer all the time and all I had to do was think a little and ask the Lord for help and he gave it to me in that way. So I took my compass out and I learned it all over again. It took some doing but it will work. It is a cheap way too, for I have an old army compass and it works real good for I took a known place and I looked for it as if I had never seen it and I came right to the spot. I made five tries and they all came out the same so it gave me the answer that I looked for.

APRIL 5

Went and bought a car. I wanted a small pickup but they wanted too much for it so I got the car instead. Now to get to the place that the map shows and see how I come out. I got here early in the morning so I have a good day to find the first spot. I looked and I looked but it took all day and I found nothing so I sat down to look at the place over good and I found nothing that even came close to the map. I then took them out of the car and went over them again. If I put them a certain way they sure looked like the same only one little thing that didn't come to me as being the same was a small mountain was not here and I could see nothing that even looked as if there ever was. There was a big wash where it was to be but there was a big wash on the old map but it was a long way from the range of mountains. I must have read it wrong. I still had a little time so I went looking

15

again and this time I could see that I had made a big goof. I had placed the sections too large so I will cut them down and see if that won't help. With this on my mind I sat down and made them smaller and put it with the old map and I got a very different reading. If I do, then I'll cut down until I get it at the right size. I was afraid of this. I should have done this before I went on this wild goose chase for I can't make too many of these kinds of goofs and it takes too much of my time. I cut it down three times and each time I did I got a different reading and I ruined the paper map so I'll have to get a different one and I'll make a thing to make the squares smaller so I don't make the paper maps in a mess.

APRIL 18

I got the things ready for the map and I am going to the cave for the maps and study them and see what I come up with. I started where I had left off and I cut the squares down twice and I started to get some very bad way off readings. I re-sectioned the larger squares and then compared it to the map, read the map again and it looked a lot better so I am pretty close to the right size so I can start all over again back to the far northern part of Utah and see what I come up with. I can see now that am going backwards. What I wouldn't give to be able to read the plates that I have and I would be able to read the map and I would have good going. But being as stupid as I am I do the things the hard way. I guess that I will always do things that way.

APRIL 20

I went and studied the map again and I got tired and did a little digging to rest. Both of them gave me no results so I gave up and went home.

APRIL 24

I ask[ed] God for some more help to see if he would lend me a hand for I am getting pretty bored with getting nothing for all my work. I went back to work to see if I could relax from it and get my mind to thinking of something different for a while. Nothing seems to work for no matter what I did today my mind came back to the maps. I must find out something that will give me the answers that I need. I can seem to see the place but it won't come to me so that I can put it into play. I just sat at the cave and thought. I did nothing just sat. I wonder if the whole thing is a joke. It is getting to seem like it is for I am not getting anywhere with it.

APRIL 26

I brought a guy by the name of Gail McCaffery up to the cave but I didn't show it to him for I didn't quite trust him. I put it to him in such a way that he had a good idea what I had. I went one way and he another and I went into the cave and I took the gold plate out and showed him and he then believed what I had told him. I made him swear to tell no one and he said that he would not but I will wait and see if he keeps his word, and if he does, maybe I'll let him in on the rest of it. If I see that he doesn't keep his word I'll just let him think that I am letting him go with me. I'll watch and see if he comes up to the cave or around it. Then I'll know whether or not to trust him.

APRIL 29

I didn't have long to wait for he came up today and brought someone with him but I didn't know the person that was with him but I'll try and find out who he is. I should have known better. You can't trust anyone. It sure makes me mad at them and myself for letting someone in on this for all they want is the money end of it. I met him down in Rick's Cafe and I talked to him and I asked where he had been and he said that he had just gotten back from Mt. Pleasant. I had hoped to see the guy that was with him but it seemed that he was alone. I found out that he drank a lot so I didn't put any more trust in him.

APRIL 30

I went to the cave and hid it so that no one would find it only me. I will have to be more careful from this day on for there will be Gail watching all the time. Boy I must be awfully dumb to pick a partner. Never again will I trust anyone until I put them to the test. I then went over west to do a little arrowhead hunting and to think things out. I must think of a way to get rid of Gail. He is a good person but this belongs to the Lord and I don't want it to *fall into the wrong hands for they will use it wrong. They will even hide it for themselves so I am back at it alone again. I found a good arrowhead grounds and, if I look, I can see the place where the cave is. I wonder if the indians knew of that place and what went on there. But I think that the people that lived there were before the indians so I guess that they wouldn't know of it as I do. I guess that they were too busy getting something to eat to think of anything else. I ask God to help me get some of these problems answered for I am getting impatient and I need something to get me back on the road.*

MAY 20

I had to spend today up at the cave for I ask[ed] for the day off to do it. I wonder what my wife will think of that if she finds out. I am mad at her any way for she went and sold some of my arrowheads for 25 cents a piece. I know that they are worth a lot more than that—at least $5.00 a piece but I worked darn hard to find what few that I have gotten any way. That's all that anyone wants is money. I can see it to get the things that a person needs but to try and get rich on something, that I don't see. I worked too hard to let her sell them for that price because they are priceless and I won't let her sell anything more of mine—I'll bet on that.

MAY 25

I got a little spare time so I came to study the maps again. I did this for the whole day but I am still as I was before—nothing. My candle has burned out so I'll have to call it a day and go home and get some more. I wonder what old Milton Harmon thinks of me getting all of these candles. I bet he thinks that I am nuts but that is the only place that I can buy them, at least the big ones. Max called and ask if I needed a job and I said that I might come winter and he said that he would keep me in mind.

MAY 27

I went to study the maps again and I drew another blank so I just looked at the things that I had. I was looking at the armor that I had found and I thought maybe I ought to go and look at the place again to see if I had left anything at the hole. For a change I would go and see if I had.

JUNE 4

I went over to the hole and I dug and found that it went in a little deeper than I thought so I started to pull myself through the small opening and I got stuck and I could go neither way so I had to move some of the dirt out from under me. While I was doing it I heard something up ahead of me but it wasn't in sight of my light so I kept on moving dirt out from under me. I looked up for something was close to my face and I looked into a rattler face. I just froze there and I couldn't move. It came closer and stopped about one-half inch from my face. This is one time that I really ask[ed] God for help for if I moved it would strike and I knew that. It then moved out of the light and I could feel it moving across my neck and up on my back. I knew that it couldn't get out the way that it had before for I was blocking the way. I sure do get into some the funniest places but this one takes the cake. The darn thing is just sitting on my back and not moving at all. It seemed like I had been here a whole night when at last he started to move and I felt him come to my neck and down across my head and then nothing. I opened my eyes and I saw the tail end of him going out of the light and I moved to the front of the hole fast. I tore my shirt and a lot of skin in doing that but I didn't want any more of that thing. I went out and got me a stick with a fork at the end and went back into the hole and I got to the back of the cave but no snakes. I felt better so I started to dig a little bit but all I could find was bones that the rats had brought in. There was nothing human there even though I thought that maybe the guy that owned the armor would still be here. But I see that he isn't and I think that he is but where? I'll just have to keep on digging and see what I come up with. I wish that I could find that snake so that I could move him outside away from here. I then could do my digging in peace but I can't see where he went. I don't see any more big holes but there are a lot of small ones. What if there is a lot of snakes here? I'll just wait and see. I sat for about an hour and I saw him at one of the holes so I let him come out towards me and I got him with the stick. I took him outside then threw him into another hole and left for home.

JUNE 9

Went to work today and decided to go up to the cave and do some more studying and see if I could see the answer that I sought. I studied for a couple of hours and gave it up for it takes too much out of me. What do I have to do to find out what I must know. I have ask[ed] the Lord but all that I seem to get is a blank. I must not be using the right approach. I know that I still have the idea that I may get rich out of this. Maybe I'll have to forget that and then I might get what I need to know. But how does a young man like me do that for that is very hard to do. I wish that I had known God and how he works but how to go about it without giving away my secret? That I don't want right now for if the Lord wanted me to he would have given me the thing that I wanted most—the answers to my questions. I dug a little more but I found nothing. I then went and looked at the cave to see what I had here for I had never looked at the cave very much. I went to the far end of the cave and I saw what I thought to be a small shelf. It was full of dust so I started to move it and I found a few more pieces of pottery and they had paint on them. I then thought that I might be able to put them together. I got all that I could find. Then I found what I think to be a bracelet of some kind. It is in the form of a snake and it is very much detailed. The length is about 1 foot long and it is coiled. It is 2½ inches wide and the head is almost 3 inches wide. I think that there may have been some kind of items for the eyes but I am not sure. The tail has got the rattles on them. It looks like something a woman would wear. When I think of these things I find that I really don't know anything at all. I am very dumb. I must seek these things out but I am not sure how to do it—another thing that I must ask God. I seem to count on him very heavily but who else do you look to. Boy, this makes a lot more to add to my ever growing collection. (When I find something I find that I sweat very much and I become very excited. I get very weak and sometimes I get a pain that hurts down deep in my back. It pulls me to the ground and I find that I cannot move for a short time until the pain leaves me. This comes, I know, from the find so I must learn to control myself and not keep getting all shook up when I make these kinds of finds. But how can a person ever find that control?) I put it with the other things that I prize above all others. I also found some more lead type things. These things I'll just put into the "X" items for I don't know what to call them.

JUNE 17

I wish that I could find out why some of these things are here. It just doesn't fit into the puzzle that I have for there have been Indians here, that I know. Now the things on the bottom must be the early generation and the ones on the top must be a later generation so I have that much straight now then who left the ones on the bottom? All that I have found have been on the bottom or pretty close to the bottom. Now what does that give me—not too much. I don't think I am missing the main part of the puzzle. My grandmother used to ask me, "I wonder what even happened to Moroni?" I'll study up on it and see if that is the one but I don't think that he was the one for I seem to come to the Jaredites. I don't know the reason that it comes to me this way but it seems to stay with me. Now, if I ask of God to tell me I might get something from him in that part. For if I read the Book of Mormon I seem to get that they did go north. I'll see what happens if I read it over and really get the inside track of the small part that was allowed to be written. I seem to feel sometimes that I am being watched. But when I check and see I see no one but the feeling will not leave so how can I find out if I am being watched. Even when I am in the cave I get it real strong but when I go outside it leaves me. I guess that it is just myself getting the wrong idea. I did a little digging with no findings and I studied the map with no help.

Here Brewer adds a footnote that the author feels should be part of this narrative:

This went on for a long time with very little help. I won't go into all the same things so I'll give all that I feel that should be said. Like the day that I got the map read and when I almost lost it all to the one of darkness. It came to be the end of my idea of getting rich out of it. I find that it does belong to the Lord and it isn't to be sold or anything gotten out of it only what is on the plates. I also found out what God can do if a person does do wrong and also that he can forgive a person but it is better for him to do as told. This will seem to be incomplete but until the Lord gives me the go ahead I'll have to keep most of it to myself. I am not to get rich from it nor am I to build myself up with it. For I lost some of God's respect when I lost some of the plates therefore I must pay the price. I won't say that I am not tempted to sell some of the items, for I could melt it down and sell the metal for a fair price but I know if I do that I will be cut off and lost. I have been told that face to face and I have been tempted many times for I have been approached by men that I knew that could have been only from the dark one for I only showed it to one man and I know that he never told anyone for I know that he had a bad fault but he was very good to keep his word. Also these men that came to me to buy, gave me the wrong name and they didn't have the right. But at that time I didn't know how to tell them. I just found out this year. So it goes to show how the Lord can protect what is his. I'll tell one of the ways that it happened to me and then you might see why I am keeping a long watch on these things. Also when I did wrong what happened to me and the ones that I *loved. I lied and I paid for that every time, but at the time they lied to me so in turn I did the same. I found that God won't allow that for no matter what, I could have been silent and been better off for then God would have protected what is his but I didn't know that at that time for I let in evil and I got the return from it. For God can and will help if he is called on. I should have been closer to him and not let my own greed get the best of me.*

JUNE 26, 1959

On this date I finally got the map read. I was down into the central part of Utah and when I came to the small section of Sanpete I saw at once that I had the map read. At least the north and south of the old map for it fit to close to be a mistake. I read it over and over to make sure that it wasn't wrong. The old map would fit only one way and that was all. That was what I was looking for. I could soon check it with the land. I would do it first thing in the morning. I felt good. Now I know that God does answer but you have to be very patient, for time means nothing to God. Time is for man and not god this I learned and I make no move without his approval and his say so for if I pass on I am sure that there will be someone that will continue on in my place and I am sure that the Lord will make the choice. I cannot tell the feeling that I have today. I have finally gotten the map read.

JUNE 27

I went out to the first location that was away from town for I didn't want anyone to see me. I took several compass readings and I started out for I would be walking a lot today. I had to find the right place and where I crossed the readings I would find the location. I think that I must find the same mark that is on the map on the earth if it is still there. I walked and I stayed on the line that I had taken with my compass. I soon saw that I should have been more careful in taking my readings for I put myself in some of the hardest climbing that there was. At the time I thought that it was going to be easy but I soon found out that it wasn't for it took all day to make my compass readings correspond but I finally did. It was sundown and I marked the spot so that I couldn't miss it and went home.

JUNE 29

I put it off as long as I could but one day I was so excited I had to see if I was right. I found the spot after looking for four hours. Now all that I had to do was find the mark. Now, what would it be on. At first I looked on the trees but after a while I sat down and decided it wouldn't be on the trees for they may not have been growing at that time so what would they use. It would have to have been here at the time and something that wouldn't move with time, something that would stay put. Now I was at a place that could have been cleaned out or washed out I don't know but I may have to do a lot of digging so I started at the place that my compass crossed and I started to dig. I dug in a small circle and started out. As I cleared out the center I put all of the dirt on the part that I had cleared off and that way I wouldn't miss anything. Now this was very hard but I couldn't think of any other way to do it, and worst of all, it took time and lots of it. I dug a hole about six feet by six feet and I had to leave for it was dark and I didn't want to miss anything.

JUNE 30

I went to the location again and I started to dig some more and at 15 feet I found the landmark. I jumped for joy for I had the map read right. I sat down filled with happiness. At long last I had read the map. Now to see what I had. I could see nothing that would even give me an idea as to what was there. I looked at the mark and I looked at the one that I had taken off the map and I saw something that caught my eye that could mean something. I'll try it and see but it pointed off a small cliff. I went off the cliff to see what was there but I couldn't see much that would give me anything to go on so I decided to do a little digging and see what came of it so I got me a long rope that I had with me and took it from the mark over the cliff and made it straight as I could. I then dug for about an hour or so and I found my first item. I was very disappointed for it was more writing on rocks. I thought that it might have been something a little more in the way of gold or even some other kind of metal but there was none. I then dug some more for there might be some that would be on some kind of metal but all that I dug up was on stone and nothing more. It soon was dark so I covered what I had so that no one would find it and went home. I'll come back sometime when I have free time. I had missed too many days now so I'll have to work overtime to make up for it.

JUNE 16 1960

I was down in the field one day and I had one of the plates with me and the hay crew was taking a rest and one of them saw the plate and ask[ed] about it. I said that I had found it and I let him look at it and then I ask him to read it and he laughed. Then one of the guys asked to see it so I showed it to him. He was more interested than anyone that I had shown before and I made him a partner. His name was Carl Poulsen from Manti. We got to talking and we made a date to go to the location. I took him up to the spot and he and I dug up some more of the same kind of plates. He then ask[ed] to keep them and I said that it was all right with me so we went home.

JUNE 17

I met Carl at the turkey coop and he said that he knew someone that could help us and he said that Mrs. Lonnie Winch of Manti knew a lot about these things so we went to her place and Carl went in and I stayed out in the car with some of the plates. I don't know what was said but some kind of meeting was made at his home so I brought some of my plates and we showed them to her. She then ask[ed] to take one of them so I let her. She ask[ed] to hear the story and I thought that if I let them know what I had they would take them away from me and that would be that so I made up a story. Then she said that she would have a Mr. Jennings of the U of U look at them. Carl said that we were to become millionaires and that did sound good at first so I then went home.

JUNE 18

I didn't know what had gone on for Mrs. Winch had stayed and Carl came to me and said that she wasn't feeling too good so maybe I would have to take them up to the U of U and I said that I would. He then said that Mrs. Winch had already made the arrangements for someone to come down and that we would soon be very rich. Then he went on to say that he knew of a big ranch that was for sale and that with the money that he was going to get he would buy it. Then it came to me at that time that I had made a big mistake. They were not mine to give. I had a feeling that I must ask of God and it was here that I got my reply. I had made the biggest mistake of all. Here I had been trusted to keep it to myself and bring it out when God said. Carl left and I prayed to God and I felt within myself that I would have to pay for this not only me but also my family would have to pay. I begged to be forgiven but I didn't get any place.

JUNE 19

I felt that I wanted to die but I called to God again and begged to be forgiven but I only got the bad news that I had to be out of the home that I was renting. I knew that it had started for homes were very hard to get. Carl came and said that we were going to become very rich but I didn't say anything for I had done wrong.

JUNE 22

Carl said that the man was to come down and look the things over and that he would let me know what happened. I was at Carl's place and Mrs. Winch came and said that the things were not good so I never said anything.

JUNE 23

Carl came and said that Mrs. Winch wanted to see me so I went and all that she did was show me an arrowhead and ask if I thought that it was any good. I looked at it but I couldn't tell if it was good for I didn't have my glass with me so I guessed that it was good but she said that it wasn't because one of her boys had made it. But I know this much that if she hadn't known that it was phony she would have guessed too, but you can tell the real ones if they have not been cleaned. Then she told me to keep my nose out of things that I didn't know anything about. They told me that the plates I had let them have would be given back at Thanksgiving but I could tell that I may not see them again. (This was what I thought would happen but why didn't they tell me to my face. This I don't understand. I was told nothing and really kept in the background.) She said that they would tell me on paper what was wrong with them. Fine, OK with me, but I didn't really care for I had other things on my mind. The first thing that I must do is go and see if they were at the location and had found the landmark, and if they had, then I knew that I might lose it all. After Mrs. Winch had her say I went to the location and I found that they had been there. I don't know what had been found for no one but me knew that they had even been up there. All my tools that I had left *were gone and the place had been gone over very good but I wasn't looking for that. I went to the place where the landmark was and I found that it hadn't been found so I was still safe. I covered it over very well and made sure that no one but me would ever find it. Why didn't they let me know of the thing that they were to do and why didn't they let me be there when the big Mr. Jennings was looking at the articles. It made me feel like I was the one that was to be the scapegoat. Well, I had ask[ed] for it so I guess I'll just have to go along with it. At least they didn't find the cave and the other things. While I was up here I again ask[ed] God to forgive me but I didn't get an answer but he showed me that he meant what he said for I had to be out of my place almost at once and I still hadn't found a place to live in. I had only one place to try and if I didn't find it to be for rent I was in very deep trouble.*

JUNE 28

I got the home but it wasn't a very good place to live in but I had to take it. We made it the best that we could and it was pretty nice after we got done fixing it up." [3]

(End of John Earl Brewer Journal)

Months turned into years, and Brewer continued to search for the answer to his ever-increasing questions that surrounded the caves. Brewer continued to trust and then distrust certain individuals that happened to fall into his good graces over the years. It was in the spring of 1974 that Brewer finally got what he wanted when he was contacted by LDS officials that a meeting was to be set up for the purpose of authenticating his claims.

From Brigham Young University was Dr. Paul Cheesman, head of Book of Mormon Studies in the Department of Religion. Accompanying him were two or three others, one of which was Elder Mark E. Peterson, of the Counsel of the Twelve. They dubbed the meeting as the first of the now "Manti Project." They headed to the town of Moroni in Sanpete County, Utah. They drove to the residence of Mormon Bishop Merlin Nielsen where the meeting was to take place. Bishop Nielson introduced John Earl Brewer to the group and then the meeting began. Brewer was a soft-spoken man and was inclined to speak so low that at times the members of the group had to lean in to hear him. Brewer told his story to the wide-eyed guests trying not to leave anything out. He explained in great detail how he found the caves and what was in them. Then he related to the group the most unbelievable story of all.

It was during one of his excavations that he uncovered a set of steps. After clearing the area of debris he found that the steps led to an entrance into what appeared to be a tomb. Upon entering the tomb-looking chamber he discovered ten objects that were covered with cedar bark. He uncovered five of these objects to find that the bark was concealing stone boxes with strange writings all over them. In the room were two large stone sepulchers which when opened each contained the mummified remains of a personage. He told the group that one had red hair with the skin still attached to the bones and that the other personage had blond hair. The mummies were very large and appeared to be a man and a woman. The man measured about nine feet in length. Brewer was asked if he had taken photographs of the mummies. To this he answered in the negative, but produced two ink sketches of the mummies that he had made while looking downward into each of their stone coffins. They had strong Mongolian features of the Chinese. Brewer stated that he had carefully catalogued the position of each artifact including the coffins. He stated that inside the stone boxes were metal plates and those were the only things that he touched because he was afraid of disturbing the mummies for fear of destroying valuable archaeological artifacts. He said the mummies had been covered with a straw-like cloth and he had only pulled it down from the heads to reveal the crown and breastplate that accompanied the personages. He also stated that shields and a sword were among the artifacts that remained in the tomb.

Sources say that Brewer reached into a briefcase and produced about 65 metal plates of various sizes, shapes and metallurgical composition. The plates were inscribed on both sides with characters of an unknown ancient writing. Some of the collection appeared to be composed of gold. For some reason Brewer would only show the gold looking plates from under the glass of a recessed picture frame. He claimed that it was for their protection.

Mr. Brewer then told the group that he had a set of plates that no one had ever seen before and that he wanted to show them to Elder Mark E. Peterson. He then produced a set of small plates with a metal band around them some five inches square. They appeared to be bronze. One small metal ring bound them on the side opposite the metal band. Elder Peterson was very impressed and suggested that the band should not be broken at that time, but the most logical moment should be in the presence of a scientific group in the proper setting with the right instruments to evaluate the archaeological significance. Dr. Paul Cheesman asked Brewer if it was possible for him to take him to the cave for the purpose of photographing the mummies.

The Mummies that Brewer discovered were never photographed. This is an ink sketch of a mummy man. This is all the proof he had of his existence.

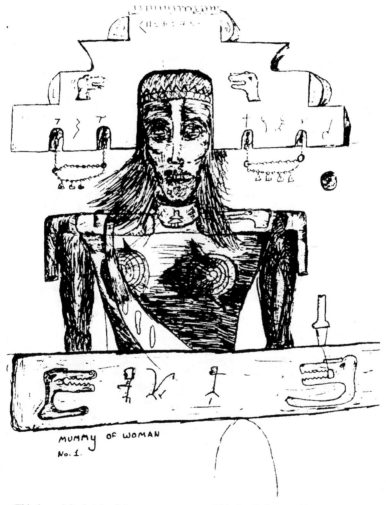

MUMMY OF WOMAN
No. 1.

This is an ink sketch of the mummy woman. This is all the proof he had of her existence.

Brewer agreed to this and added that the entrance would have to be enlarged as Dr. Cheesman was a rather large man. He further agreed to allow an archaeological team from the Brigham Young University to follow up after Cheesman had a chance to visit the cave for further evaluation.

Time passed and the planned visit by Dr. Cheesman never materialized. Brewer had lost faith is those very men he had waited on for so long to give him all the right answers. Sources say that the reason for this was because certain turn of events prevented Brewer from keeping his word with Dr. Cheesman. Brewer had gone to the cave to think things out as he had done so many times in the past. It was on one of these trips to the chamber that he felt the presence of another person in the room who held a light, and his first impression was that he had been followed. He was told by the person that he was not to take anything from the cave for personal gain, whereupon he was seized by a force of power that threw his body to the ground and left his consciousness looking at his body from above. While in this state the person introduced himself as Ether, an ancient spirit. The personage explained that he was not to seek financial gain from the things in the chamber and that he was to protect the discovery. He was told that LDS Church authorities should be informed and aware of the discovery but not be involved at this time. Brewer told the personage that he was not worthy to be a custodian in as much as he liked to smoke and drink a little and was not active in the church. He was told that he had "other attributes" and was to be careful in protecting the contents of the cave.

It was shortly afterwards that the Brewer story leaked out to the newspapers. On November 26, 1975, in the year following the meeting with Dr. Cheesman and Elder Peterson, an article appeared in the Deseret News in Salt Lake City, entitled, *"John Brewer has a Cave but He's not Giving Tours,"* edited by staff writer Dale Van Atta. He quoted Dr. Jesse Jennings of the University of Utah Archaeology Department as stating that the sandstone tablet which the University of Utah obtained from Brewer was a "ridiculous hoax." Dr. Ray Matheny, BYU archaeologist, was even more critical. He was quoted as saying he had "wasted his time exposing the man's works. It was a clumsy attempt to perpetrate a fraudulent claim of antiquity." Only Cheesman was quoted as to having mixed feelings, " They could be real."

This article embarrassed Brewer and he felt betrayed. He was determined not to have any further dealings with BYU officials. Although he retained a respect for Dr. Cheesman he avoided any further contact by church or university-sponsored officials. He would not share his discovery with any one.

It was during the summer of 1975 that Brewer became acquainted with a man who was an anthropologist. (It should be noted here that the author has omitted this anthropologist's name from the record for reasons of privacy, and has in place of his name used only his last initial.) Dr. H. had lived in Manti for almost nine years and had come to know Brewer through a BYU professor named Rodney Turner, who had told Dr. H. that John had some interesting copper plates that had been dug from an old cave near the town of Manti. Dr. H. then started to become acquainted with Brewer at his home during that summer. He listened with interest to Brewer's story without reflecting much emotion or judgement. He was allowed to look at the plates but did not ask questions about the cave or location of the discovery. In short, he was very low key in his approach to Brewer.

Dr. H. revealed to this author that he even helped Brewer at the turkey plant late at night dressing the foul smelling-birds. He did anything it took to get next to Brewer and to get him to place his trust in Dr. H. He stated that he liked Brewer and that Brewer had a charm about him that was genuine. Over the following months a keen friendship developed between the two men. They became very close friends and spent many hours hiking together in the mountains east and west of Sanpete valley. Brewer would sometimes get upset at his new friend because the simple atmosphere was at times interrupted by Dr. H. discussing life and philosophy. It was during this time that Brewer told Dr. H. of his stone map indicating the location to a second cave somewhere within Sanpete County, Utah. After months of figuring out the points of direction given on it, Brewer eventually found what he had been looking for. Dr. H. explains in his own words :

> When he had gained enough confidence in me, he invited me to go with him high up in the mountains just south of Wales, Utah, where this second cave was. From it were taken different artifacts bearing a striking similarity to Maya art work from Mexico and Guatemala. Again, as with the first cave behind the Manti Temple hill, heavy cemented stone boxes weighting approximately ninety pounds each and highly decorated with ingenious art work, were removed. Within these boxes were also found ancient metal plates of curious workmanship. The stone boxes had been carefully enclosed in a juniper bark wrapping with pine pitch smeared all around so as to make them relatively waterproof.

When Brewer finally allowed Dr. H. to see the inside of the second cave, they had been meandering on the hillsides when suddenly Brewer stopped and told Dr. H. to take off his shirt and pants so he could squeeze into a tunnel and see the chamber they had so often discussed. Dr. H. did as suggested and followed John into a tunnel that had been dug on a downward track, barely squeezing and squirming like a worm through the narrow passageway. After a short distance he came to an opening, and reaching down felt the edge of a set of stairs that led into a chamber. The chamber was about twenty feet long and fourteen feet wide. The air was stifling and breathing was very labored. Several inches of fine dust covered everything, and puffed up with each step that they took. About twenty-five stone boxes were stacked against one wall and another twenty against the other wall. Most were wrapped with a cover of juniper bark with pine pitch smeared all over them to make them waterproof. In a smaller chamber were two mummies of large stature. Dr. H. describes the mummies:

> The texture of their skin was soft, almost moist, like tanned leather. In the cave I saw an abundance of weapons, swords, tools, copper and metal plates of various sizes, all of which were very curious. Some of the copper, plates were of a strange composition, shattering like glass into fibrous pieces, not unlike the windshield of a car, if dropped. I believe that this chamber houses at least two different ages of antiquities.

Dr. H. concludes that Mr. Brewer believes he is a special custodian of the contents of the chamber, that he is being very careful with whom he deals with and to whom he divulges any information as to the contents and whereabouts of the chamber. On several occasions, Dr. H. and Brewer visited the cave, but only once during daylight hours. The chamber was very warm during this daytime entry and Dr. H. claims that a winter visit is more comfortable than a summer visit. This would suggest that the chamber is not deep into the ground and that the temperature is regulated by outside weather forces. This and privacy account for the visit at night.

Brewer decided to finally show Dr. H. his discoveries in the other cave. After a very difficult journey, Brewer and Dr. H. finally reached the well-hidden cave entrance hidden under an overhanging ledge with a small crawl space underneath. Again, the contents of this cave were stone boxes and plates containing strange writings, curious weapons and tools. On one wall of the cave were petroglyphs depicting a hunting scene. On several of the stone boxes were Mayan-type head glyphs or drawings. Dr. H. decided that this was the work of the second age. It was a large cave with several areas of exploration leading into tunnels and rooms. Many of the stone boxes weighed from sixty to ninety pounds and could not be easily removed and brought from high on the mountain. Dr. H. stated: "The cemented stone boxes were highly decorated with ingenious art work. Within the boxes were metal plates of curious workmanship." With great effort, a few of the boxes and their contents were brought off the mountain. Dr. H. has several of these in his possession. He also has a large number of the metal plates in his custody that this author has inspected.

John Brewer gave two boxes to Dr. Paul Cheesman. Sometime later Brewer brought Dr. H. several of the plates and asked him to translate them for him. Brewer informed Dr. H. that he had been instructed to bring the plates to him, that he was the logical person to whom he could direct this request. Dr. H. told Brewer that he was not qualified nor capable of this feat and told him, "You know John, there is a devil. You need to be careful." In an interview by the author Dr. H. stated:

> I was caught up with the mystic of the adventure. I sought for a prayerful answer for assistance by the Spirit. I believed what Brewer had told me. The thought came that if I had faith I could translate." He states, "At no time was I able to decipher or read the plates from the characters that were upon them. I neither read from the right to the left, nor from the top to the bottom, nor did I understand the particular meaning of each character. With no Urim and Thumim I gave myself to prayer.

Dr. H. stated that he discovered he was able to understand the meaning of the plates through a thought process that came to him from without, and through the spirit he began to decipher the writings upon the plates for a short period of time. He claimed that a conscious of a presence of power was taking over his mind. A divine intelligence helped him to translate the plates. After he translated the plates he turned them back over to Brewer who showed great interest. Dr. H. told this author that the plates are filled with beautiful and wonderful doctrines. He went on to say that at no time did he ever pretend to read the plates although he came to understand some of the method in the writing. He stated that he was amazed at the ability of the ancients to express an idea or a story within an ideogram containing only a few strokes. However, this was to become a source of serious difficulty a few months later.

For reasons which Dr. H. does not care to discuss, the relationship with John Brewer took a hard turn that resulted in his loss of friendship with Brewer, who told him abruptly at their last meeting, "Get away from me you devil!" When questioned about Dr. H's association with Brewer he stated:

During the period of my close association with Brewer, I never knew the man to lay claim to reading or interpreting any of the ancient symbols or writings that appeared on the outside of these stone boxes or any of the plate inscriptions either. As for myself, I can only say that they are of very ancient origin (with those in the second cave being some centuries "newer" by reason of their "fresher" appearance) and that the artifacts in Cave No. 2, found with the help of the stone map in Cave No. 1, strengthen the evident cultural links which existed between the Jaredites (Olmecs) and the amalgamated Zarahemlites/Nephites/Lamanites (Maya).

Beyond this, however, one cannot venture too far lest ridicule from the academic profession and Utah's major religious entity be heaped upon him. Brewer had more than his share of it, and later on when I became temporarily affiliated with him in his archaeological extravaganzas, I too received the blunt end of criticism from jealous ecclesiastical and academic authorities, who felt that as a devout member of the Mormon Church and an active participant in the scientific community, I had simply "wandered off track" and needed to be reined in. Since my religious membership and academic livelihood were involved, I was "persuaded" (read nicely forced) to leave well enough alone and tend to my own business of medical anthropology.

Whatever happened to Brewer after this fateful 1980-81 ultimatum was handed down, I never learned. Nor have I been in touch with the man since then, although still retaining in my private collection enough artifacts from both caves to convince the most doubting skeptic that in those hidden caves laid precious treasures and sacred records which rightfully belong to those of Native American ancestry.

The fact is that Dr. H. was disfellowshipped for a period of one year for behavior unbecoming a Latter-day Saint. This stemmed from fraud and misconduct with a woman. The High Council court listened to and acted upon several other charges of a personal nature that were brought up against Dr. H.'s membership in the LDS Church. He moved from Manti and returned to Salt Lake City, Utah with other members of his immediate family. He was told by his father to conclude his relationship with Brewer and the chamber, and not to return to the site. "You were brought in by invitation, do not go back into that cave." For a period of time he complied with this fatherly advice but curiosity getting the best of him he did return a few years later. As he entered the chamber he discovered that most of the stone boxes were missing. The size of the original collection and the obvious inability of any-one to remove them without being discovered left him with the strong impression that a greater force had removed them for safer keeping. Dr. H. believes in ancient spirits, map stones, John Brewer, and his own ability to translate ancient records. Ray Matheny, Ph.D., and William James Adams, Jr., M.A., read a paper at the Twenty-Second Annual Symposium on the Archaeology of the Scriptures at Brigham Young University on the 28th of October 1972. The title of their paper was "An Archaeological & Linguistic Analysis of the Manti Tablets." The report is as follows:

> On January 20, 1970, Clyde Pritchet of the Zoology department brought to me four tablets made of light colored limestone, each containing a Semitic-like inscription. In order that we might not overlook any important discoveries that could provide us with more information on the scriptures of the New World, an investi-gation was made of these tablets.

> The owner of the tablets (name withheld) claimed to have found them sealed in the earth in an archaeological context. He said that he had hunted for arrowheads in the Manti area for many years, searching the same places repeatedly, always finding new things. One technique that he used was to turn over flat rocks and look under them for concealed arrowheads which others had not thought to do. He claimed to have been using the above technique two years previous to our investigation along the west bank of the Sevier River, a few miles northwest of Manti, Utah. Under a stone which the owner of the tablets lifted up he saw two flat stones sticking upright out of a small depression of the ground. He fur-ther stated that he had dug these stones up and discovered that they had peculiar markings on them. This discovery further stimu-lated him to dig at the spot to about "waist deep" where he found the remainder of the tablets.

> On January 21, 1970, Clyde Pritchet, Dale Berge of the Anthropology and Archaeology department, James Walker of Photographic Services, and myself went to the spot where the owner of the tablets claimed that he had found them. We thor-oughly examined the earth and found a shallow depression.

Excavation at that spot showed clearly that the earth there had not been disturbed and consisted of shallow topsoil overlying what appeared to be Pleistocene gravel. We encountered a large stone about one foot below the surface, which was well rounded from stream course action and which had not been moved since it was naturally deposited there. We dispute the claim that a recent excavation had been made at the spot where the owner of the tablets says he found them. Also, we dispute the claim that any archaeological context existed for the two upright standing stones. There simply was not any evidence for any excavation having taken place by man at the place claimed.

LABORATORY EXAMINATION OF THE TABLETS

The tablets are light brown in color and are slightly lighter in hue than the stones found in the Manti Temple. The temple stones have been exposed to the atmosphere for about 80 years and have turned darker with time, although some stones have remained a light hue, or were lighter when quarried. Some fresh scuff marks appear on the surface of the Manti Tablets exposing a whitish lime-stone. The inscription of the thickest stone (71-40., Chart I) is not as fresh as the scuff marks on the surface, but contains fine sand.

The stones were cleaned only in part in order to maintain control over observation. Cleaned parts of the inscription reveal that they are lighter in color and fresh looking. The surface color is darker and suggest that it was prepared some time before the inscriptions were made.

Inscription marks are so distinctive that they must have been made with a hard metal tool. A low power binocular microscopic examination shows that a sharp tool was used gouging out the stone in successive strokes. A deep center gouge is visible along with two to three gouge marks on the slope. A radius in each end of the gouge of the marks shows tool entry and exit. A dash on the top line of one tablet was made by pressing the cutting implement into the stone on the right side, and then moving it to the left. Other marks examined are not as clear as this one to indicate the mode of tool movement.

36

Metal is found on the surface of the thick tablet that appears to be solder or lead. No metal particles are found in the gouges of the inscriptions, indicating that an extremely hard metal tool was used in cutting the stone. Experiments show that mild carbon steel leaves traces of metal on lime-stone when it is pressed hard on the surface, but that stainless steel, such as that used for dental picks, leaves no trace.

Workmanship of making the inscriptions is not of a high quality, but has produced irregular marks. These marks suggest the difficulty in making them and shows that the engraver lost patience on occasion.

Two of the four tablets were partially coated with pine pitch obscuring some of the inscriptions. The pitch was thick and did not seep into any of the inscription marks. White bleached cotton fibers are found impressed into the pine pitch. The cotton appears fresh and not old. One tablet shows the weave of cotton cloth impressed into the pitch. Pitch on both tablets is hard and brittle. Pitch must have been soft when first wrapped in cotton cloth. Pine pitch is honey color and is not darkened and cracked from age, nor does it show evidence of exposure to moisture and soil for a long period of time.

The pitch was easily dissolved by soaking in zylol for a few hours in order to expose all of the inscriptions. The fast action of zylol further suggests recent treatment of the tablets rather then a long term interment in the soil as claimed.

From the technological point of view I conclude that the tablets are of recent manufacture, using modern tools.

OTHER TABLETS FROM THE MANTI AREA

In 1964 several limestone tablets bearing Semitic-like inscriptions were shown to me which were found in a cave near Manti. These tablets are in the museum at the department of Anthropology, University of Utah. They contain inscriptions similar to those described above.

Examination of these University of Utah tablets suggests recent and clumsy manufacture with crude drawings in addition to inscriptions.

Recently inscribed lead tablets were brought to my attention that were supposedly found in the mountains near Manti. These lead tablets contain a small script similar to that of the stone tablets reputedly to have come from the same area. Interestingly, the same person who found the four inscribed tablets discussed herein also found the lead plates.

I think that it is clear that someone is in the business of manufacturing inscriptions in the Manti area for his own entertainment in hopes of exciting the Latter Day Saints into some foolish action. The inscriptions found on the tablets have their own story to tell.

LINGUISTIC ANALYSIS
by William James Adams, Jr.

I wish to thank the symposium committee for this invitation to discuss the Manti Tablets in conjunction with Dr. Ray Matheny. I also wish to thank two graduate students—Paul Jesclard for preparing the autographs and LeGrand Davies for preparing frequency sign lists. Finally, I wish to thank the College of Religious Instruction for the financial aid they gave me.

After Dr. Matheny's archaeological analysis, the burden of the language falls on me. Following the archaeological suggestion of a fraud, the first approach was to search for authentic inscriptions which the forger could have copied. Because of the Semitic-like appearance of the inscriptions, a search of Palestinian inscriptions was made.[5] This proving fruitless, Bemotic and Hieratic Egyptian were considered. This again proved fruitless. I then sampled the writing systems of the world often finding a sign or two like the signs in the Manti Tablets but never an exact comparison and no authentic inscriptions which could have been copied. In America the Manti Tablets were compared to such inscriptions as the Davenport stone, The Kinderhook plates, etc, but again no direct comparison.[6] Thus, from this exhaustive search, I must conclude that the Manti Tablets contain an inscription which is unique in and of itself.

With this development, the second approach was that of decipherment. Here I followed the techniques used for decipherment's in the past—such as that used by Champollion in deciphering Egyptian, by Grotefend and Rawlinson in deciphering Akkadian, and by Ventris in decipherment of Cretan Linear B.[7]

The first problem in decipherment is the direction of writing. It might be good to envision a type-written page of English. The margin where we begin to read from is straight whereas the other margin is ragged. (Here William Adams Jr. explains several charts that he is showing during the symposium, explaining the margins of these charts.)

With the direction of writing determined, the next step indicated by past decipherments was to prepare "frequency sign lists." For this purpose I found Tablets 1 and 2 most alike and Tablets 3 and 4 most alike. Tablets 1 and 2 contain some one hundred signs and Tablets 3 and 4 contain some two hundred signs. From this I concluded that the script was representing syllables (syllabic) and was not an alphabetic script.

The next step is to note the groupings in which the individual signs cluster. This has been one of the major keys to past decipherments. Champollion noted clusters which he assumed were Egyptian names, Rawlinson noted clusters which he assumed meant "NAME, king of kings, lord of lords, king of the whole earth," and Ventris noted clusters of signs at the ends of words in lists he assumed were Greek case endings. This key of clustering is well illustrated in Chart VII. This is part of the Code of Hammurabi and contains about as many signs as one of our Manti Tablets. The whole code is written with about 250 different signs. In the upper corner are two signs read as a-an. The cluster is repeated twice more as indicated. Part way down the right column are two signs which begin the line and are read i-na. This cluster of signs is repeated again near the bottom of the right column as indicated. As I looked for repeated clusterings of signs in the Manti Tablets I found only the dash and triangle seen near the end of Line 3, Tablet 1 and near the middle of line 4, Tablet 1 (See Chart 1.)[8] Now, as I have noted, authentic scripts have frequently recurring clusters of signs. This is even true of authentic scripts so far undeciphered such as Cretan Linear A. Years before

Rawlinson deciphered Akkadian, Grotefend had noted the clusterings I have noted on Chart VII. But with these Manti Tablets, I have been able to find only one cluster of two signs repeated twice. What then can we conclude from this situation? From a language point of view I believe that we must conclude that the Manti Tablets are not authentic and thus a fake. Instead of a meaningful script, we have here the haphazardous and meaningless scratchings of a forger and frauder. Thus, as a scholar of languages, my conclusion is in full harmony with the archaeological conclusions of Dr. Ray Matheney.

(End Report by Matheny and Adams)

It was not enough that this report had discredited John but now six months later he was again accused of fraud by a couple that had first believed his incredible story. After a short visit with Brewer the couple sent the following statement to Dr. Paul Cheesman:

13, APRIL 1973

We, Carl Poulsen and Louise A. Poulsen, do solemnly swear the following to be the facts. (1) I, Carl Poulsen, have known John Earl Brewer for approximately eight years. (2) I, Carl Poulsen, went with John Earl Brewer to dig for artifacts west of Manti, Utah.(3) We witnessed under Brewer's matress several pieces of stone partly inscribed plus a pocket knife. When confronted with the accusation that he had frauded the ones under the mattress and the ones I, Carl Poulsen, had found with him West of Manti, he, John Earl Brewer had no comment and shrugged off the accusation.

Signed
Carl Poulsen, (and) Louise A. Poulsen

71-40., CHART 1

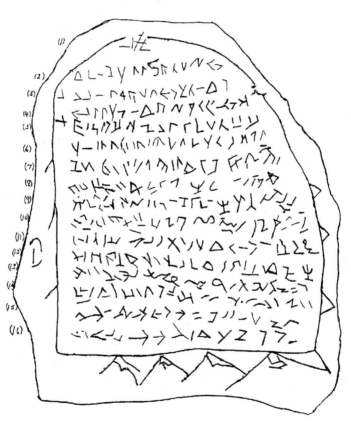

41

MANTI LEAD PLATE #2

MANTI LEAD PLATE #4

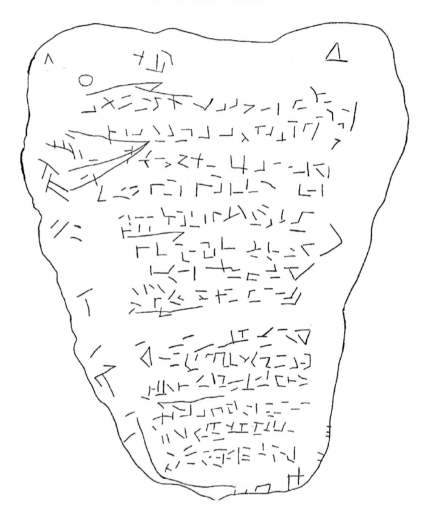

MANTI LEAD PLATE #5

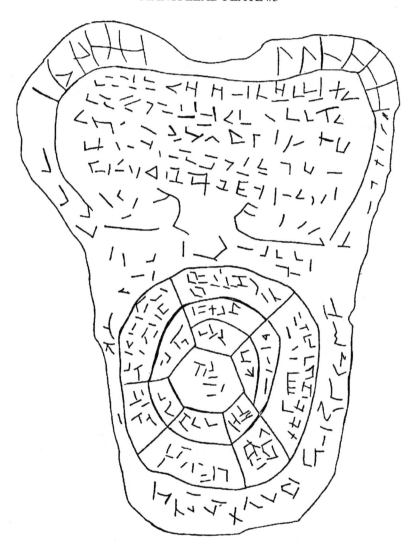

CHART #2 OBVERSE

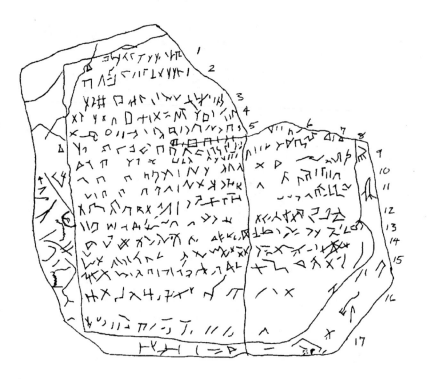

CHART #3 OBVERSE

CHART #3 REVERSE

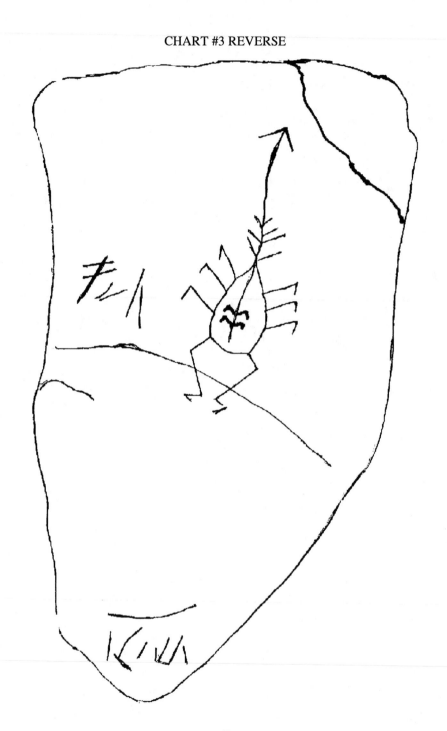

CHART #4 OBVERSE

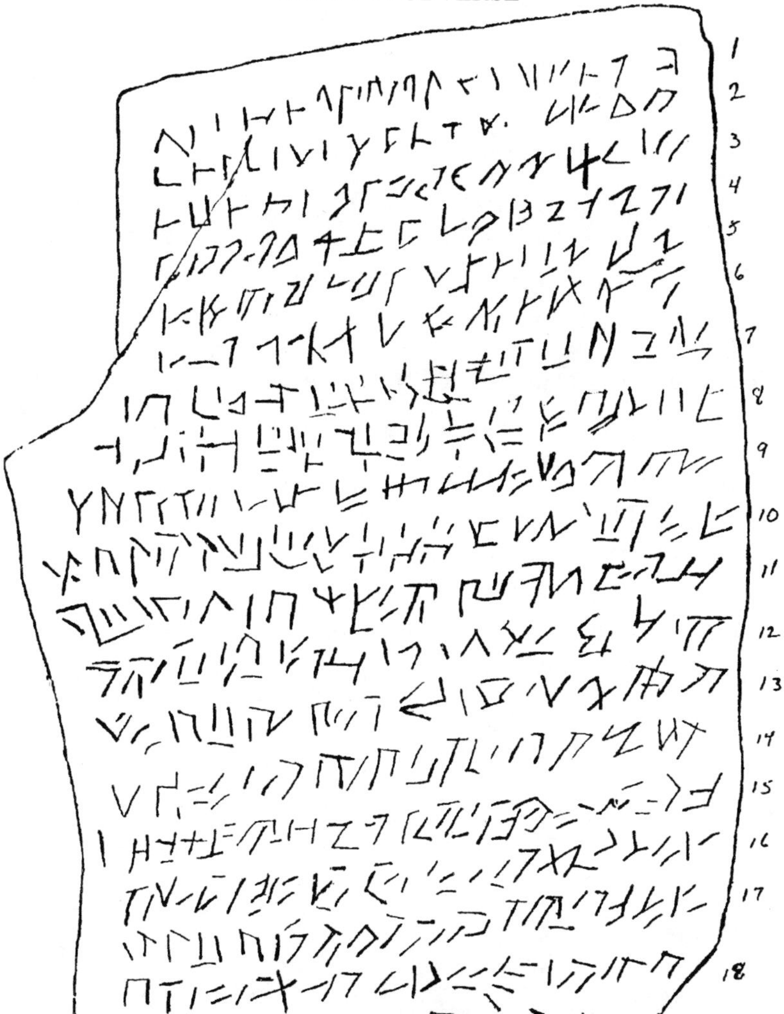

CHART #4 REVERSE

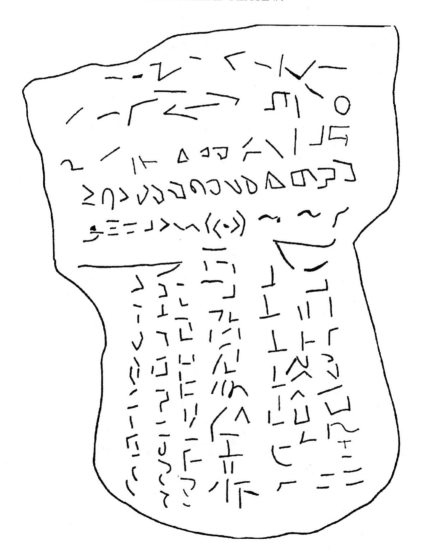

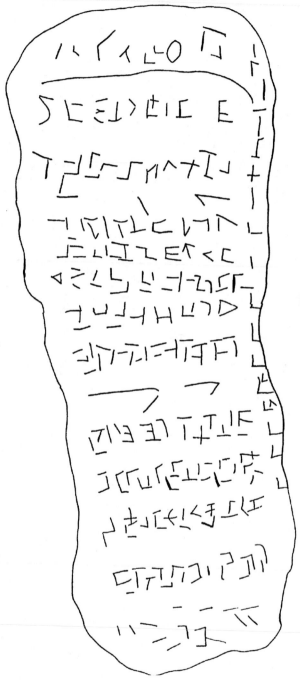

The mystery that surrounds the Manti Tablets and the mummies may never be solved. Did Mr. Brewer fabricate tablets to throw people off track because he felt that he had betrayed the trust of the angel that visited him? Was he really just leading people on and bringing discredit upon himself for a kind of punishment?

Did Mr. Brewer fabricate the whole story? Evidence leads one to believe this is not the case. True as it may be, Mr. Brewer did fabricate some of the tablets that he turned over to certain individuals, and true he led some university personnel to a location that was not the actual location of recovered artifacts. He had his reasons for doing this. Did John Earl Brewer have a cave? Did Dr. H. have the gift to translate the tablets? Were there two giant mummies? The questions mount as the mystery grows.

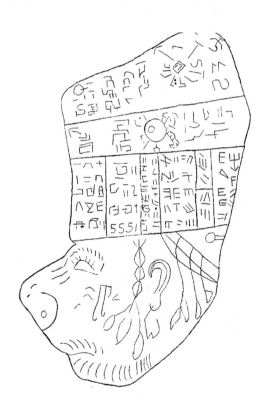

This figure is made of pure gold according to one source and fits in the palm of the hand. An actual photo could not be obtained, but witnesses have been interviewed and authenticity has been proven.

The first photograph ever taken of the copper tablets taken from the tomb of the giants. Several hundred of these small tablets still lay within the depths of the old cave near Manti, Utah.

The same smaller box shown on the previous picture.

Below are some of the larger stone boxes.

A stone box with the plates.

Shown above is one of the smaller stone boxes with some of the cedar bark wrapping still attached.

Shown above is one of the larger stone boxes. Notice how snug the tablets fit inside.

FOOTNOTES

1. Temple hill petroglyhps. Manti, Utah.
2. Antonio de Reinaldo maps of 1851-1853. Map in Author's possession.
3. John Earl Brewer's Journal. Copy in Author's possession.
4. Personal Interview with John Heinerman Ph.D. 1993.
5. Diringer, David, *The Alphabet*, Vols. 1 & 2 and Hans Jensen, *Sign, Symbol and Script.* translated by George Unwin (New York: J. P. Putman's Sons, 1969).
6. Burgon, Glade Lynn. *An Analysis of Purported Ancient Linear Inscriptions.*
   Brigham Young University: (Unpublished Dissertation, 1972).
7. Friedrich, Johannes. *Extinct Languages.* (New York: Philosophical Library, 1975).
8. Harper, Robert Francis. *The Code of Hammurabi.* (Chicago: University of Chicago Press, 1904), Plate VI.

CHAPTER 2
THE KINDERHOOK PLATES

The story of the famous "Kinderhook Plates" has raised eyebrows throughout the country for years. It was Robert Wiley, of Kinderhook, Pike County, Illinois who had three dreams in succession that there was a buried treasure near his home. The dreams were so implanted in his mind that he had a hard time thinking of anything else. He even thought that he was losing his mind. In the dream he saw that the treasure was in a mound of sorts. And in each dream he was directed to this mound where he would dig to find the treasure. It was a strange occurrence for Wiley, and he wasn't sure what to make of it.

On the 16th of April, Wiley followed the directions of his dreams to a mound not far from town. He labored most of the day in opening a shaft some ten feet deep, but had to abandon the project when it began to rain. He returned on the 23rd of April with several others, including two Mormons, to resume the digging. Upon arriving at the mound, the men engaged in excavating the site where Wiley had begun his operation. It was hard work but the men with Wiley had believed his story and were very enthusiastic about what lay ahead of them deep within the bowels of the mound.

After several hours of digging, the men uncovered charcoal and bones. While moving the charcoal and bones out of the hole, one of the men found a layer of limestone that had decayed grass imbedded in it. This was very odd. Digging still further, they encountered some sort of clay bricks that appeared as if they had been strongly burnt. Under the layer of bricks they found more bones. They appeared to be human and they were also burnt. Within this layer they found a bundle of six brass plates, joined together by iron bands that crumbled at the slightest touch.

One of the group was the town physician, Dr. W. P. Harris. It was agreed by all that he should take possession of the tablets, so that they could be cleansed with a solution of dilute sulfuric acid. The group was elated to find that the plates contained some sort of ancient writing. Shortly after this time, the leader and prophet of the Mormon Church, Joseph Smith Jr., was contacted and told about the Kinderhook find. In his personal journal he records the following:

MONDAY, MAY, 1

I rode out with Lucien Woodworth, and paid him 20 P. for the Nauvoo House, which I borrowed of William Allen. I insert fac-similes of the six brass plates found near Kinderhook, in Pike county, Illinois, on April 23, by Mr. Robert Wiley and others, while excavating a large mound. They found a skeleton about six feet from the surface of the earth, which must have stood nine feet high. The plates were found on the breast of the skeleton and were covered on both sides with ancient characters.

I have translated a portion of them, and find they contain the history of the person with whom they were found. He was a descendant of Ham, through the loins of Pharaoh, king of Egypt, and that he received his kingdom from the Ruler of heaven and earth.[1]

John Taylor, editor of the *Times and Seasons*, could not hold back when this article was published in the *Quincy Whig* that challenged Joseph Smith to translate the writings on the plates:

By whom these plates were deposited must ever remain a secret, unless someone skilled in deciphering hieroglyphics may be found to unravel the mystery. Some pretend to say that Smith, the Mormon leader, has the ability to read them. If he has, he will confer a great favor on the public by removing the mystery which hangs over them. A person present when the plates were found remarked that it would go to prove the authenticity of the Book of Mormon, which it undoubtedly will.

The plates above alluded to were exhibited in this city last week, and are now, we understand, in Nauvoo, subject to the inspection of the Mormon Prophet. The public curiosity is greatly excited; and if Smith can decipher the hieroglyphics on the plates, he will do more towards throwing light on the early history of this continent than any man now living.

I quote the following editorial from the *Times and Seasons*...then John Taylors rebutted it.

Circumstances are daily transpiring which give additional testimony to the authenticity of the Book of Mormon. A few years ago, although supported by indubitable, unimpeachable testimony, it was looked upon in the same light by the world in general, and by the religious world in particular, as the expedition of Columbus to this continent was by the different courts that he visited, and laid his project before. The literati looked upon his expedition as wild and visionary, they suspected very much the integrity of his pretensions, and looked upon him—to say the least—as a fool, for entertaining such wild and visionary views. The royal courts aided by geographers, thought it was impossible that another continent should or could exist; and they were assisted in their views by the learned clergy, who, to put the matter beyond all doubt, stated that it was contrary to Scripture; that the apostles preached to all the world, and that as they did not come to America, it was impossible that there should be any such place. Thus at variance with the opinions of the great, in opposition to science and religion, he set sail, and actually came to America; it was no dream, no fiction; but a solid reality; and however unphilosophical and infidel the notion might be, men had to believe it; and it was soon found out that it would agree both with religion and philosophy. So when the Book of Mormon first made its appearance among men, it was looked upon by many as a wild speculation, and that it was dangerous to the interest and happiness of the religious world. But when it was found to teach virtue, honesty, integrity, and pure religion, this objection was laid aside as being untenable.

We were then told that the inhabitants of this continent were and always had been a rude, barbarous race, uncouth, unlettered, and without civilization. But when they were told of the various relics that have been found indicative of civilization, intelligence, and learning,—when they were told of the wealth, architecture, and splendor of ancient Mexico,—when recent developments proved beyond a doubt that there are ancient ruins in Central America, which, in point of magnificence, beauty, strength, and architectural design, vie with any of the most splendid ruins on the Asiatic Continent,–when they could trace the fine delineation's of the sculptor's chisel on the beautiful statue, the mysterious hieroglyphic, and the unknown character, they began to believe that a wise, powerful, intelligent, and scientific race had inhabited this continent; but still it was improbable–nay almost impossible, notwithstanding the testimony of history to the contrary, that anything like plates could have been used anciently, particularly among this people.

The following letter and certificate will perhaps have a tendency to convince the skeptical that such things have been used and that even the obnoxious Book of Mormon may be true. And as the people in Columbus' day were obliged to believe that there was such a place as America, so will the people in this day be obliged to believe, however reluctantly, that there may have been such plates as those from which the Book of Mormon was translated.

Mr. Smith has had those plates, what his opinion concerning them is, we have not yet ascertained. The gentleman that owns them has taken them away, or we should have given a fac-simile of the plates and characters in this number. We are informed however, that he purposes returning with them for translation, if so, we may be able yet to furnish our readers with it.

It will be seen by the annexed statement of the *Quincy Whig*, that there are more dreamers and money-diggers than Joseph Smith in the world; and the worthy editor is obliged to acknowledge that this circumstance will go a good way to prove the authenticity of the Book of Mormon. He further states that "IF Joseph Smith can decipher the hieroglyphics on the plates, he will do more towards throwing light on the early history of this continent than any man living." We think that he has done that already in translating and publishing the Book of Mormon, and would advise the gentleman and all interested to read for themselves and understand. We have no doubt, however, but Mr. Smith will be able to translate them.

The original source of Joseph Smith's statement under the date of May 1, 1843 concerning the Kinderhook plates has never been located. It has been discovered that much of Volume V of the *Documentary History of the Church* was recorded by Leo Hawkins in 1853, after the saints arrived in the territory of Utah, and was compiled by Willard Richards from journals. The Kinderhook story was not found through examination of the journal of Willard Richards.

An undated letter over the signature of W. Fugate, one of the men that discovered the Kinderhook plates, states: "We understood Jo Smith said (the plates) would make a book of 1200 pages but he could not agree to translate them until they were sent to the Antiquarian Society at Philadelphia, France, and England. They were sent, and the answer was that there were no such hieroglyphics known and if there ever had been they long since passed away." Then Smith began his translation. All of the following periodicals indicate that the Kinderhook plates were being sent to the Antiquarian Society after May 1st, 1843; *Times and Seasons*, May 7, 1843; *The Prophet*, February 15, 1843: and the *Nauvoo Neighbor*.

Jules Remy, in "A Journey to Great Salt Lake City," recorded a slightly different version of Joseph Smith's claims regarding the tablets and translation, and quoted his source as Joseph Smith's autobiography. The *Times and Seasons, Quincy Whig* and the *Davenport Gazette* each ran stories discussing the existence of the six Kinderhook tablets and printed the affidavit of the nine men verifying their authenticity. These publications appeared during the lifetime of Joseph Smith, and there is no word from Joseph Smith either refuting the facts in these articles or condoning them. A letter dated December 9, 1843 from Frances Markon to J. J. Harding of Washington attests to the existence of the tablets and indicates his wishes to display the tablets in Washington, D.C. Mention is made of the Kinderhook tablets but no reference is made to their being a hoax or fraud.

The tablets were returned to Robert Wiley in Kinderhook who eventually gave them to Professor McDowell to be displayed in the McDowell Museum of St. Louis, Missouri. The museum was ransacked by the Second Iowa Reserve during the Civil War and many of the contents were stolen or destroyed under the quise of war. The tablets disappeared at this time and also from the public's interest. The sketch of the tablets remained an enigma among the few Mormon people who were aware of the discovery.

Twelve years after the discovery of the tablets, and after the death of Joseph Smith, W.P. Harris wrote a letter to a Mr. Flagg, dated April 25, 1855, which remarked, among other things:

> But since that time, Bridge Whitten said to me that he cut and prepared the plates, and he and R. Wiley engraved them themselves, and that there was nitric acid put upon them the night before they were found to rust the iron ring and band. And that they were carried to the mound, rubbed in the dirt and carefully dropped into the pit where they were found.

The most shocking news came when, in an affidavit dated June 30, 1879, some thirty-six years after the finding of the Kinderhook plates, W. Fugate made the following known to Mr. J. T. Cobb:

Mound Station Illinois

R. J. T. COBB:

I received your letter in regard to those "plates" and will say in answer they are a humbug gotten up by Robert Wiley, Bridge Whitten (a blacksmith), and myself. B. Whitten is dead, Wiley may be living, he was a Missourian. None of the nine persons who signed the certificate knew the secret —excepting Wiley and myself. There were two Mormon Elders present where the plates were found, their names were March and Sharp. A man by the name of Sarage (of Quincy) under an assumed name borrowed the plates of Wiley to show to his friends there and took them to Jo Smith, after they were returned. Wiley gave them to a Prof. McDowell of St. Louis, Mo. for his museum, but since McDowell's death, we heard they were taken to Chicago Medical College and placed in the museum. By visiting to Prof. John Hodgen of St. Louis, Mo. you may find out where they are and also if Wiley is still living. He was a graduate of that college—Wiley.

Dr. Harris was not a Mormon, he was a chemist and he took the rust off the plates when found—Dr. is dead. Wiley was not a Mormon. The plates were cut out of copper by a blacksmith (Bridge Whitten). Wiley and myself made the hieroglyphics. A man by the name of Jeronian saw the plates before they were put in the mound, but whether he is living or not; I do not know. I do not know any man by the name of Roberts. I will say in conclusion that the plates were made simply for a joke. I believe, I have answered all your questions, and given you the particulars concerning them.

Yours respectfully,
W. Fugate

P.S. As father is too old and nervous to write, he requested me to answer, and the above is written as he directed.

Matthew Fugate

From the writing of the above letters through the year 1929 there are various interpretations of the historical path of the Kinderhook tablets. Reed Durham has compiled two possible explanations of the period. According to his findings, one of the tablets is authentic and one of them is not. Also in 1929, M. Wilford Poulson discovered that the Chicago Historical Society Museum might have in its possession one of the original Kinderhook tablets.

An interview with Dr. Carl Furr in Provo, Utah, 1969 revealed that he had examined a Kinderhook tablet in Chicago during the years 1936-37. He commented that the tablet he had seen in Chicago appeared to be different from the one later on display at Brigham Young University. He thought the tablet in Chicago had been punched. He did not recall the acid splotch on the BYU tablet as being there previously, and he remembered the tablet was thicker than it is now. His opinion was that it had been etched with acid, and even the present analysis had not changed his mind.

James H. Breasted, an Egyptologist from the University of Chicago, said in 1914, "The Kinderhook Plates" are, of course, childish forgeries, as the scientific world has known for years." We are not told upon what basis Mr. Breasted made his claim. Was he looking at the characters from the printed facsimiles or the original tablets?

On the 25th of June, 1953, two engravers from Chicago analyzed the tablet at the Chicago Historical Society, and concluded that the tablet was engraved with a pointed instrument, and not etched with acid. Dr. Welbe Ricks wrote an article in the *Improvement Era*, September 1962, in which he summarized his findings concerning the Kinderhook tablets and included the affidavit.[2]

Dr. George M. Lawrence, a Princeton physicist, conducted a physical study of one of the Kinderhook tablets and published a limited number of copies. His conclusions were that the tablet was brass, and acid etched. It was also his opinion that it could have been made in 1843. Subsequently, in March and May of 1967, Dr. Lawrence sent letters to the Chicago Historical Society, reporting the discussion between himself, Mr. Edward J. Puriski, and Mr. Stanley B. Hill, the two engravers who had signed the affidavit to the effect that the tablets were engraved with a tool. As a result of the discussion, all parties held the same convictions as before.

On October 16, 1969, Dr. Paul Cheesman of the Brigham Young University submitted the Kinderhook tablet that had been on display at the University to the University of Utah Chemistry Department Laboratory for an x-ray fluorescence test. A section of the tablet on the nonacid splotch side was made. The results of this test, as interpreted by William Dibble of the Physics Department of Brigham Young University, showed that the tablet was generally 80% copper and 20% zinc which would make the composition brass. Traces of small amounts of chrome, iron, tin and lead were also found.[3]

During the month of October 1969, a rubbed sample of the metal of the Kinderhook plate was sent for a Neutron Reaction test to the University of Michigan. This neutron activation analysis consists of irradiating the sample by a nuclear reactor. The amounts and types of radio isotopes produced are determined using nuclear radiation detection equipment. This provides information about the sample's elemental composition. With regard to authentication, the results become more valuable when compared with elemental composition of several specimens authenticated already which are similar to the sample in type and in time of fabrication. A report dated March 4, 1970, from the Department of Chemistry at the University of Michigan, revealed that the test samples of the Kinderhook plate were "quite consistent in their impurity levels and contain the highest level of impurities..."; hence they are old copper or brass.

The reports on the authenticity of the Kinderhook plates continue to pour in, as well as the reports of fraud. If the Kinderhook plates were a fraud, why the odd bell-shaped plates? Why would anyone go to the trouble of making facsimiles of a fraud? The plate from Chicago may be an unusual authentic Indian mound artifact found in situ, or it may be a fake made by a village blacksmith in Nauvoo. It may be a copy of one of the original Kinderhook plates. If this Kinderhook plate is authentic, then it is the first known pre-Spanish tablet found in the New World known to this author. Letters sent to Eastern museums and historical societies, especially in Chicago, inquiring if they had ever examined the Kinderhook plates, have so far been fruitless. Because of the similarity of brass and bronze, these metals are sometimes identified erroneously by observers. Time holds a key to this and many other studies. If the next forty years generate many new archaeological discoveries and more sophisticated means of analysis, we may have more precise answers.

But why did Fugate falsify his statements made in his letter to Cobb that he, Wiley, and Whitton had executed a bizarre plan; that they had in fact made the hieroglyphics by making impressions on beeswax and filling them with acid and thus etching the six copper plates which they buried thirteen feet deep to play a hoax on their friends? He claims the plates were cut from modern copper while all other parties to the discovery signed an affidavit that they are made of brass. The plate in the Chicago museum is brass. His story also declares that they bound the plates with a strap of pig iron, and then covered them with a thick layer of rust. It would have been no small feat to have the pig iron disintegrate into dust at the touch of a human hand. Why dig a thirteen-foot pit into a mound to plant the plates when a few feet would have been satisfactory to satisfy a spurious find?

Fugate was not telling the truth in regards to his association with the plates. It took seventy-four years to find one of the Kinderhook plates to refute his story. Letters have been written to museums and private collectors for years throughout the country in an effort to locate a bell-shaped plate. Dr. F. C. A. Richardson, M.D. said that he had seen two such plates, and that he had erroneously tabbed it as, "A plate of brass known as one of the only two recognized original plates of the Mormon Bible.

THE KINDERHOOK PLATES

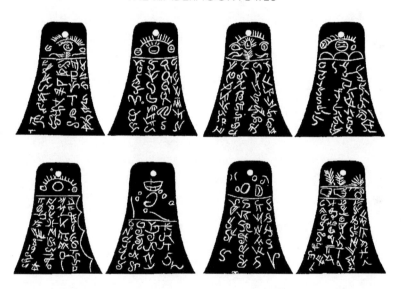

FOOTNOTES

1. Smith, Joseph. *History of the Church of Jesus Christ of Latter-day Saints* (Salt Lake City: Deseret Book Company, 1951), vol. 5, p. 372.
2. The notarized certificate of Stanley B. Hill and Edward Pwiiske. (Copy in author's possession.)
3. Lawrence, George M. *Report of a Physical Study of the Kinderhook Plate Number 5.* Princeton, May, 1966.

CHAPTER 3
THE MIDDLE BRONZE AGE TABLET OF THE WASATCH

The Wasatch mountains of Utah extend north to Brigham City and south to Mount Nebo in central Utah. They are a magnificent range of mountains, with high granite ledges inhabited by Rocky Mountain goats, bighorn sheep, mule deer, elk and other animals. The beauty of this range of mountains is beyond description and is admired by all who feast their eyes upon their snow-capped peaks. One wonders what the first settlers thought when they beheld those lofty mountains. Hunters, fishermen, campers, hikers and skiers ramble up these mountain slopes by the thousands each and every year, and seem to cover every nook and cranny. But this is really not the case. There are hundreds of little side canyons that seldom see a human in them. There are hundreds of little groves of trees that go unnoticed for years on end. This was the case when a certain young man happened into one of these secluded spots during the hunting season of 1989.[1]

A cool autumn wind blew into Johnny's face as he headed for his father's truck. It was early, too early for a young lad of just nineteen years. But, it was hunting season, and he had been waiting all year for this day, and a little cool wind was not going to stop him from going out into the mountains for a trophy buck. Johnny Clarke was an average young man. He had not graduated from high school yet, but he was working on a G.E.D. so that he could land a better-paying job than the one he now had. Johnny sat in the center while his father sat at the wheel and his uncle Bill took the right seat. They were to meet a cousin at the mouth of Parley's canyon at 4:30 a. m., and then from there they would head into the mountains. Johnny could hardly wait to get there, but they did arrive on time and soon they were convoying up the highway to a secret spot that his cousin had spotted while flying over the area two weeks before.

It was still dark when they arrived at the end of the road. They parked their trucks and then fumbled around in the dark for their guns and packs. It would be a strenuous hike. They didn't know the area that well, so they relied on the cousin to guide the party into the secret side canyon that he'd seen. Soon they were on their way, winding up a faint game trail through quakie trees and dead fall, going slowly so that they would not fall. They left the quakies and entered the pines as the night slowly began turning into day. The trail widened, and then narrowed, and soon they were up on a ledge of rock looking down into a small canyon that was covered with pines. They couldn't quite see the bottom of the canyon yet, so they had to wait for the sun to climb higher into the sky. The bottom of the canyon was a grassy meadow with a small spring in it—a great place for a trophy mule deer. The party sat on the ledge and decided how they would hunt this hidden canyon. Uncle Bill and Cousin Dan would work their way around the canyon to the other side, and then at a given signal they would move into the canyon below. Once they were on the move into the canyon Johnny and his father, Richard, would make their move over the ledges into the canyon.

It seemed like an eternity before Dan and Bill made it to the other side. Uncle Bill waved his hat to signal the descent into the canyon below, so without further delay they began the hike. Moving slowing with his rifle at the ready, Johnny moved with a delicate grace through the trees, an art he'd learned by watching his father over the years. His father moved to the left and out of sight of Johnny, but within ear shot. Johnny would walk for a short distance and then stop and glass the area below. He'd watch the trees and stare into the foliage waiting to see the faintest movement. He was constantly aware of the location of the other hunters.

All of a sudden, there he was—a giant buck deer, right below Johnny, watching the other hillside and his ears were straight ahead picking up the sounds of the two men across the valley. The big buck didn't even know that Johnny was on top of him until it was too late. Johnny dropped to one knee, held his rifle steady, and then gently pulled the trigger. The blast rocked the morning silence sending camp robbers out of their hidden nest in the tops of the pines to safer places. "Did you get one?" yelled his father. "Yea, a big one," Johnny yelled back. Hurrying down the mountain Johnny raced to the downed deer. He had hit him right in the heart, killed him on the spot. The deer had come to rest on the edge of another granite ledge. Another foot or so and he would have tumbled down almost to the bottom. Johnny was wishing he had, because he'd have to drag him down there anyway to bone him out for the hike back out. Soon Johnny was joined by his father and between the two of them they field-dressed the animal to make it easier to handle. Johnny got in front of the big 4-point buck and began pulling him over the ledges towards the grassy meadow below. As he was pulling the deer, he would look for upthrusting rocks to place his feet to prevent him from falling. All of a sudden, one of the rocks he had selected to stand on gave way and down Johnny went. The deer came tumbling down with him and the next thing he knew he was under the deer but unharmed. Johnny scrambled from under the deer and looked up to where the rock had dislodged itself. He could see a square hole and from where he was standing it didn't look natural. He decided to look into the hole for one reason or another, or maybe just to see why the rock had come out so easily.

Johnny worked his way up to the hole made by the dislodged boulder. He examined the outside area of the hole and then peered into the dark square-shaped hole. His eyes adjusted to the darkness and he could see that the hole went back in much further than he first thought. He then noticed something, an object, leaning up against the side of the hole. It looked square and had a shine to it. Reaching in, Johnny retrieved it and brought it out into the light. It was the strangest thing he had ever seen. He called to his hunting companions to look at this strange object. It looked to be about four inches long and about three inches wide, with a thickness of not more than a quarter of an inch. The men could see that it had some figures etched into the surface and with a closer examination they could see that it was a tablet or plate of some kind with some very old and odd writings all over one side. They became very excited and began a frantic search of the immediate area in the hopes of finding yet another cave or small hole. Not only did they search for more caves and holes, they turned over every rock that would budge. Finding nothing more, the men turned their attention back to the deer hunt. Johnny secured the plate in his backpack and began the arduous task of getting his trophy mule deer off the mountain.[2]

Upon returning home, Johnny took the plate and set it on the table. He stared at the plate for some time, first wondering how a thing like this found its way into a small square cave, and why there? He wondered who made such an object, and why. He could do nothing more than that, just sit and stare, and wonder. He noticed that it was dirty, and had a strange film over it. He also noticed that some of the markings were covered with a crystal-looking material. Not knowing any better and being unschooled in this type of work, Johnny decided to clean the plate to see if that would enhance the markings on it. He began with different abrasives, and naval jelly. It was clean by now, and to his dismay he found that he had damaged the tablet by some of the cleaners he had used. Not knowing what to do with the new-found object, he decided to take it to his neighbor, James Morrison, to see if he could tell what it might be. He also wanted to know how much the thing was worth, believing that it was silver and worth some money. James looked at the tablet and then suggested to Johnny that it may have some sort of historical value besides. Johnny was uncertain what to do with the tablet now, so he asked James to find a buyer for him and that if he did in fact find someone they would split the money down the middle. James agreed and soon had possession of the tablet. He decided to take the plate to the Church of Jesus Christ of Latter-day Saints to see if any of their people could help in finding out what this strange plate was. After a day in the "high rise" in downtown Salt Lake City, Morrison was no closer to an answer than he had been the first time he laid eyes on the tablet. Morrison then decided to take the tablet to a friend of his that might help him in getting the answers he needed. Mike Savage was a big man, and had a hobby collecting memorabilia of past and present day 'giants.' He had always had in interest in ancient artifacts, and when Morrison brought the tablet to him, Mike was very excited. He suggested that the tablet be taken to the Utah Historical Society as well as the University of Utah.

Within a few days, Mike Savage was visited by his uncle Ross Butler, who showed an intense interest in the tablet. Savage gave Butler permission to seek out Morrison for the purpose of making a photocopy of the tablet. After Butler had accomplished this, he sent the copy to an old friend, Prof. Willaim Hartley, at the Smith Institute of the LDS Church, located on the campus of Brigham Young University, Provo, Utah. When Professor Hartley looked at the photocopy, he was hesitant. He had seen many fake artifacts and papers, and this could very well be just another one. Hartley searched out a colleague of his for another opinion, Dr. Deloy Pack of the Department of Asian and Near Eastern Languages at BYU. On November 11, 1989 Hartley sent Pack a type-written letter with a hand-written note at the top of the page:

Dr. Pack, Will Griggs said you'd be the one to run this probable $3 bill by Something to bother you. Can you give me a response, & send back a photocopy.

Thanks
(signed) Bill Hartley
135KMB

Memo: 11. 21. 89
To: Pack
From: Bill Hartley [3]
Re: Supposedly recently found plate with ancient writings

Knowing how easily fake and phony things get circulating, I hesitate to run this past you. But, just in case there is anything to it...Third hand, for what its worth.

...

Ross Butler, an elderly man for whom I am writing a family history, obtained this copy, Xerox copy, of what he was told is a small metal plate. Story he heard was that a deer hunter from SLC very recently slipped on a rock up one of the canyons and when the rock unloosed, this plate was jarred loose and came out. Imprint in ground from the plate was there where the rock was.

Ross learned about it through relatives, one of whom is Michael Savage. Ross said that the man who found it is neighbor to (James) Fred Morrison of Fred Morrison Printing Company on 4th East and 21st South in SLC, northwest corner.

Apparently the finder or this Fred Morrison, one of the two, took this plate to the Church Historical Department and were told that the man who might be able to help them was on vacation until after Thanksgiving. (Who in the world would that be?)

And that's all I can tell you, based on 3rd hand information.

This is Ross Butler's only Xerox copy and he would like it back. I have made no copies of my own yet.
What do you think? [4]

(signed) B.H.

PHOTO OF THE TABLET

Sometime later William (Bill) Hartley received a handwritten response back from Deloy Pack:

Bro. Hartley,

Just a quick response to the photocopy you sent me.The photo appears to be of a clay tablet, rather than a metal plate—note how the characters at the end of the lines sometimes appear to be going around or onto a curving edge. Also, the top and bottom appear to be rounded rather than flat. Without seeing the original one can not be sure that this isn't simply a photo of a clay tablet taken from some book.

As far as the writing is concerned, I am not able to read it. This may be because it is too damaged or because it's been too long since I've done any reading in Aldiodion.

There are no obvious mistakes such as wedge signs going the wrong direction. The cross sign 'X' at the beginning of a couple of lines looks a little strange and the general shape of the signs appears to be later than one would expect for the time of the Jaredites. (Here one sentence of the letter is unreadable). Someone bringing the cuneiform script to America.

Naturally, since I can't read it, I can't say whether it is genuine or not. You ought to consult Paul Hoskisson for another "expert" opinion.

I am returning your copy with this response.[5]

(signed) Deloy

Deloy Pack did as suggested and aquired another 'expert' opinion from Professor Paul Hoskisson, Ancient Studies, Brigham Young University. On December 4, 1989 Hoskisson sent the following letter to Bill Hartley:

Bill Hartley
Smith Institue for Church History
135KMB
BYU

Dear Bill,

In regard to the photocopies of a supposed metal tablet with writing on it and the accompanying letter you sent me, without seeing the original it would be impossible to say anything for sure. But allow me to make some general observations.

If the photocopies accurately render the look of the original object, then there are serious problems. A few of the shapes of the signs and their placement seem amateurish (see what appears to be an 'A' sign on line 5 and the strange signs on either side of the lacuna at the end of line 9). Deloy Pack pointed out some of these in his reponse. In addition, some of the signs seem to be so sloppily done that I would almost have to rule out a scribe trained in the cuneiform schools. The ductus of the signs would point to the Middle Bronze Age or at the latest the Late Bronze Age (see the DINGER sign on line 12 and the beginning of line 14). Chronologically this would present problems with any known migration from the Old World.

Unless the original could change my mind, I would have to say that the photocopies are of (a) poorly made modern copy of a Middle Bronze Age tablet(s).With the hope that this has been useful I remain,

Yours,
(signed) Paul Hiskisson[6]

After this information had been sent to Ross Butler and then on to Mike Savage, an old friend of Mike's came to see him. Rod Livingston was a retired dentist and when he was told of the tablet and how it was acquired he became instantly interested. Rod, with Mike's approval, went straight to Morrison. After the meeting, both men arranged to meet with Johnny Clarke to see if an arrangement could be made so that Rod could take possession of the tablet in order to research its origin, at his own expense.

Livingston dove into this work headlong and worked hard to find an answer to this puzzle. He contacted people with impressive credentials such as Dr. James F. O'Connel, Center for Archaeological Research; Dr. Phil Hammond, Middle East Studies; Dr. Milton Wadsworth, Dean, School of Mines; Dr. Charles Pitt, Department of Minerals & Metallurgy; Dr. Adrade Joy, Material Science; Dr. Erick Peterson, Department of Geology & Geophysics, plus several others. These renowned experts performed numerous tests on the plate including X-ray defraction, electronic scanning microscope, electron prose, florescent analysis, spectron neutron activation, micro-probe analysis, laser spectrograph, and a chemical analysis. The tablet was found to be made from a natural unrefined ore consisting primarily of the following elements:

SYMBOL	ELEMENT	PROPORTION
AG	SILVER	MAJOR
NI	NICKEL	MINOR
CU	COPPER	MINOR
ZN	ZINC	TRACE
SB	ANTIMONY	TRACE
PB	LEAD	TRACE

Electron microscope photographs of the tablets engravings.

Microscopic examination revealed crystal deposits and malachite (CU_2, CO_3, OH_2) in the bottom recesses of the cuneiform symbols. This then ruled out the possibility that the plate was of recent manufacture, as these deposits would suggest a minimum age in the hundreds of years. Dr. Phil Hammond, University of Utah, proved very helpful to Livingston. During his long career Hammond had examined 50 similar cuneiforms tablets except for two differences. They had all been clay, and none were this old. He recognized many of the symbols but not enough to read the tablet. However, he felt that the plate was around 4400 to 4600 years old, and is an example of the very earliest cuneiforms.

Dr. Hammond wrote a letter to one of his former students, and enclosed photocopies of the tablet. This student now heads the Ancient Studies deptments at Yale University. Dr. Marvin Young is supposed to be the best authority in the United States on early cuneiforms. The two men corresponded back and forth for some time. Dr.Young asked for the plate to be sent to Yale for tests that would take approximately three weeks and instructed the shippers to insure the tablet for $20,000.00. With photocopies in hand, Dr. Young made more copies and sent them to a Professor Albertine Gaur at Oxford, England. Gaur is the world's best and foremost authority on the study of ancient cuneiforms. He stated that if it is what it appears to be, and is genuine, it is one of the earliest cuneiforms, and one of only ten such cuneiforms known in the world on metal tablets. He was most anxious to see it.

Several other reputable people have examined the tablet and each one responds a little different than the other. The noted master of Egyptian language at Brigham Young University, Hugh Nibley, examined the tablet and then dismissed it as a fake resembling the Soper/Savage collection.

During the summer of 1990, I was told about the tablet and soon a meeting was set up between Mike Savage, Rod Livingston, two others and myself. Livingston had heard that I had been researching signs and symbols for some years and wanted to know if I could help him in deciphering the symbols on the tablet. The meeting was held at the home of Rod Livingston and proved to be quite interesting. The only markings that I had ever seen used in researching old Spanish symbols and Indian petroglyphs was the sign of the cross. It was apparent that the symbols were much older than what I had been led to believe at first. I took a special interest in the tablet and began to research the possibilities of its origin. With Rod and Mike's permission, I began to search out individuals that might help in this work. I came upon many dead-end leads. Then one afternoon I remembered a man whom I had met years ago, an intellect in Hebrew studies. I made a phone call to his home and arranged for Mike Savage to bring the tablet down to Woodland Hills, Utah, where we would show it to Avraham Gileadi. Gileadi is a Hebrew scholar and literary analyst and holds a Ph.D. in ancient studies. His education includes rabbinical school in Jerusalem, religious and scholarly pursuits at Brigham Young University, and graduate work in biblical languages and literature at the Toronto School of Theology in Canada. Once the formalities were over, the tablet was brought out and given to Gileadi. He spent a few moments in deep thought, turning the tablet over and over, examining it thoroughly. Then he turned to us and said, "This is cuneiform writing, and it is very old." He then asked Mike where it came from. Mike told the story, leaving out the exact location. Gileadi then looked at it again and then told us that it was Jaredite. He then gave Mike a list of men to contact so that they, too, could look at the tablet and perhaps give more insight to the knowledge already gleaned. From that meeting others were set up. Dr. John Heinerman, Ph.D. and author of several books including one titled, *Spiritual Wisdom of the Native Americans.* expressed great interest in the tablet when told about it. After several hours of inspection and reproduction of the tablet, Heinerman, too, pronounced the tablet Jaredite.

The late Dr. Paul R. Cheesman would have been the logical one to have seen this tablet. Since that was impossible, I brought his old partner and friend, who had traveled with him all over the world in search of ancient writings and artifacts, to the home of Mike Savage. J. Golden Barton is a man of medium frame, white hair, and very knowledgeable, having spent so much time with the noted Dr. Cheesman. Barton examined the tablet and was under the impression that it was left here by Jaredites. He then reminded us that the earth once was one mass and that if the tablet was nearly 5,000 years old it could have always been here.

Still uncertain of the authenticity of the tablet, this author sent a photograph and a brief explanation as to how the tablet was found to H. B. Nicholson, professor of anthropology at the University of California, Los Angeles. Professor Nicholson has studied the peoples of Mesoamerica for almost 40 years. He has also uncovered ancient records of those people under a temple in central Mexico. His response was as follows:

April 9, 1995
Mr. Shaffer;

I received your letter and photographs and was excited to read that this tablet was found in your fair State. It is not at all hard to understand how this tablet found its way to that remote canyon. It is safe to say that people from the central America area and even further south made treks into the northern parts of what is now North America. It is also evident that they carried with them records of their histories as well as of their ancestors. I have seen Cuneiform clay tablets taken from temples in Mexico as well as South America. I must say that I have not heard of tablets made of Silver like the one in your photograph. It was most likely made of clay first and then cast into the silver tablet. It would suggest that the record it bares is of value or the makers would have left it in the natural clay form.

I plan on coming to the University of Utah this summer and will look you up that I may see this tablet first hand. In the mean time I am sending you a couple other names that may be able to shed more light on this tablet.

(signed) H. Nicholson [7]

With this report my thoughts of this tablet being authentic seems more than likely. The search continues, however, and with the evidence piling up it is very possible that the answer will be forthcoming.

FOOTNOTES

1. The location where the tablet was found cannot be revealed at this time at the requests of the owners of the tablet.
2. The names of the people involved in the finding of the tablet have been changed at their requests. The canyon and locations have also been changed.
3. Copy of letter in author's files. Jack Welch records.
4. Copy of letter in author's files.
5. Copy of letter in author's files.
6. Letter in author's files.
7. Letter in author's files.

CHAPTER 4
THE UNKNOWN NATION

In 1993 I had the rare opportunity to meet and to be befriended by a man who is described simply as "extraordinary." The name of this gentleman cannot be divulged because of his position and his acquaintance with many scholars and university professors. I was introduced to this man by another exceedingly gracious man, who I, too, describe as genuine.

One summer afternoon while visiting "Gary" (their names have been changed to protect them) in Ogden, Utah, he made mention to me that he had a friend that would love to see and hear about my on-going research of the presence of the Spanish in Utah, and would like to hear what I had to say about the ancient inhabitants before the Spanish. A meeting was set up for the next day. We were greeted by "Paul" and his wife at their door in a quiet, well-dressed neighborhood in north Provo. After the normal formalities, I was asked to express my views and opinions on the topics mentioned above, which I did with vigor and in great detail. All the while my small audience sat quietly with eyes fixed upon mine, fascinated with what they heard. After I had finished, Paul spoke up and said that he agreed with all that I had said and that he, too, had a fascination with the records of the past. As time went on, my new friend became more at ease with me and soon let me see some artifacts that were simply amazing. He said he could see that I could be trusted or he wouldn't have ever let me look at those things. He then brought out a large box full of small manila envelopes. He told me that what he held in these small manila envelopes were the original negatives once belonging to Elder Milton R. Hunter of the Church of Jesus Christ of Latter-day Saints. I asked how he obtained these negatives to which he responded, "Elder Hunter gave them to me for safe keeping, and admonished me not to let them out of my hands." I was then handed the box and told that I could view the negatives, which I did. What I saw was truly a testimony builder. There in my hands were the photographs of ancient tablets that proved that this continent was inhabited long before any Spanish came upon its shores. Not only were the tablets inscribed with ancient writings, they were also carved to depict events surrounding the lives of these people and their beliefs. The night passed quickly as we looked at the negatives and discussed the story surrounding the discovery of the tablets. From that day on my new friend and I have been on several outings that were very gratifying.

As time passed, I proceeded to explore the story of the tablets and how Elder Milton R. Hunter came to photograph them. In April of 1960, two men, Elder James Bird and Elder Paul Roundy, were assigned as missionaries in the South Bend, Indiana area. One of their contacts was the Reverend Charles E. Sheedy at the University of Notre Dame. The missionaries were teaching the story of Joseph Smith and his receiving the records of the Nephites and how they were engraved on brass and golden plates. While engaged in their story, Father Sheedy interrupted them and commented that he had something to show the two young men. "What is it that you have to show us?" asked Bird. "I have some of the same type of tablets that you are talking about," remarked Father Sheedy. This immediately aroused the curiosity of the two missionaries. The priest took the young duo to the attic of the O'Shaughnessy Building where he uncovered three crates. Out of one of the crates, he removed several slate and copper tablets covered with hieroglyphics, pictographs, and strange inscriptions. This excited the two young men and they exclaimed to each other that here was proof of ancient people on the continent. The missionaries thought that finding these tablets, and knowing that there was a connection with the story of the golden plates, many people in the area would be converted. That was not how things turned out.

Father Sheedy did not want to be converted, nor did he want the missionaries to convert his faculty or students. What he wanted was someone to authenticate, or to disprove, the value of the collection. He thought that perhaps the Mormons could help in some way. Not knowing what to do with their new-found knowledge, the young men decided to let the matter rest with a higher authority. After they had returned to their apartment, they wrote a letter to Elder Milton R. Hunter of the First Quorum of the Seventy in Salt Lake City, Utah. They never received a reply. What had happened was nothing more than human error. Elder Hunter had accidentally misplaced the letter. When he finally discovered what had happened, two years had passed. He knew that by now the two missionaries were long gone. He decided to write a letter to the Reverend Charles Sheedy at Notre Dame and ask for an appointment to visit with him.

During this time, more tablets were being offered to add to the collection. One such offer came from Ellis Soper in North Carolina. He had a large collection of similar artifacts and seemed very anxious to get rid of them. Notre Dame did not have the space nor the desire to except the Soper collection. After the meeting between the Reverend Charles Sheedy and

Milton R. Hunter, it was agreed that Hunter would take the collection back to Utah for further study. Hunter was excited about the collection. He was an historical archaeologist by avocation, and had written several books in an effort to substantiate and supplement the Book of Mormon claims.

Father Sheedy was uncertain as to the value of the collection, and therefore suggested that they be on loan to the Church of Jesus Christ of Latter-day Saints for the purpose of study only. Later on, this was made an outright grant and the church authorities were now back in the business of plates and tablets inscribed with hieroglyphic writings.

Before Milton R. Hunter saw the collection, a Miss Henriette Mertz, a devoted Catholic, Chicago attorney, and by avocation author and historical archaeologist, had previously discovered the dusty artifacts in the attic at Notre Dame University. She was granted permission to examine the tablets. For six years she studied and examined the tablets and when she was finally finished she promised that a book would result authenticating the collection. It was found out later that the publisher had disapproved the manuscript partly because of spurious charges against the collection. He thought that the ancient Greek-Egyptian origin theory of Mertz's was bizarre and the whole affair was going nowhere and might lead to some embarrassment for Notre Dame. It seemed that the best thing to do was to encourage the university to "dump" the collection before a charge of fraud was heard.

Miss Mertz had done her homework. She pieced together the history of ancient America as she saw it, and how she saw it was not far from right. Over time, settlers who pushed into the frontier told in their records and journals of the discovery of ancient ruins and strange artifacts that were found when forests and lands were cleared for the plow. The settlers found old mine tunnels and smelters, they found rusted armor and weapons of war. Some of the relics were of Indian origin, and some were of the Spanish conquistadors. But by far the greater number of artifacts were from a civilization of a by-gone age that has defied identification. Along the Mississippi River and its tributaries are found evidences of what archaeologists call "the Mound Builders," because of the large, strange mounds they left behind which suggested an important part of their society. Archaeologists believe that the mound builders were Anglo Saxon, and a cultured race of people not related to the American Indian as we know them. Whoever these ancient people were, they left behind some very interesting and puzzling remains. The number of mounds and their size, including the area of land that they once covered, shows evidence of a great achievement.

Not only do the mounds cover the Mississippi drainage, they have also been found in Utah, Arizona, Nevada and Idaho. Some have had artifacts buried inside them while others have not. It is estimated that there were over nine thousand sites alone in the state of Ohio, and Michigan had over one thousand sites. Historians believe that these ancient people were highly cultured and had an advanced civilization with an organized political and military structure. The people were educated in art, writing and metal work. Some modern-day Indian tribes tell in their legends of a white civilization that had been here long before they came. However, the scholars of our day do not share in the belief that the mound builders were an unknown white race of people who were highly civilized. It is interesting to consider the circumstances that led to the abandonment of this theory as a myth. The fact is that by 1890 the tide of opinion had shifted, and men of science denied that there had ever been a highly-cultured white race in America's past. This very radical turn-about came as the result of the scientific leadership of Mr. John Wesley Powell. It was in 1897 when Congress created the Smithsonian Institution's Bureau of Ethology. Major John W. Powell, a Civil War hero, and an influential man, received additional power and prestige as the Bureau's first director. He was disposed to think that the mound builders were the ancestors of the Indians. He made his theory known in the Bureau's first annual report, published in 1880, which states:

> That the vestiges of art discovered do not excel in any respect the arts of the Indian Tribes know[n] to history. There is, therefore, no reason for us to search for an extra-limital origin through lost tribes for the arts discovered in the mounds of North America.

Powell was born within a few miles of Palmyra, New York. His father was a Protestant and had little use for the new Mormon Church. It may have been that some bias had crept into Powell's theory. It wasn't long before Powell's theory was accepted in the community as fact. Even scholars and historians who had once backed up the finds as credible had now changed their minds and began to favor Powell's theory. One writer was quoted as saying:

> Evidence contrary to Powell's stated opinion was explained as fraudulent, as buried in the mounds intrusively, or simply re-interpreted to favor the new theory. From this time forward, anything that referred to the original glorious Mound Builder theory was considered mythical. It was a very hostile academic environment for anyone who ventured to propose that there had ever been a highly civilized group of people in the New World.

Records in Edmore, Michigan tell of a James O. Scotford, who while building a fence dug up a large earthen casket. Scotford took the casket back to town and told the story of how he found the casket, and how it was hidden in the bowels of a strange mound. Within the next few weeks people from the town went in search for more mounds and artifacts. By summer's end, over 500 mounds, all covered with trees and other vegetation, were uncovered. There were hundreds of artifacts found, including other earthen caskets, clay and copper tablets, arrowheads, spear points, jars, and much more. All were very beautiful and most, if not all, articles were carved and engraved with historical scenes, biblical scenes, and strange symbols. One newspaper reported:

So many citizens from the towns of Wyman and Edmore were eyewitness and involved in the excavating and recovery of the relics and the evidence so clear that doubts were never entertained for a moment as to the authenticity of the work. In one case a casket was found under the roots of a tree which by its concentric circles was shown to be about 300 years old; and one of the roots of the tree had grown through the corner of the casket and was coiled up inside the box, but so decayed that it was broken with a touch.

The reports of relics continued to pour in as farmers plowed and cleared ground for crops. The activity mounted as more relics were found and soon Montcalm County in Michigan was covered with excavations. One man that became very interested in the mounds and what they held was the Reverend James Savage, Pastor of the Roman Catholic Church of the Most High Trinity in Detroit. After he had excavated several mounds, he described them as follows:

On these mounds you may find large and aged trees, oaks, pines, and other varieties. The decayed roots of pine and other trees that grew, thrived and died on these mounds are there. They contain another peculiarity. There is a stria of charcoal and ashes in each mound. This stria often shows the basin shaped contour of the interior of the mound when its possessor was laid away at rest. There does not appear, as a rule, sufficient charcoal and ashes for cremation, only enough for purification. In some mounds, however, there is a heavy stria. These prehistoric mounds of Michigan contain caskets, lamps, bowls, pipes, tablets, etc. of clay: battle-axes, knives, spears, daggers spades, etc., and a variety of ornamental wearing apparel—all of chilled copper; stone tablets, medallions, metals, skinning knives, various implements and of strange design, the object of which we can not imagine. One remarkable feature of these mounds—they contain no flint implements of any kind, nor have I seen any stone or copper beads; other ornamental wearing apparel is frequent.

It was further stated that:

Many curious things were unearthed, such as caskets, tablets, amulets of slate stone, cups, vases, alters, lamps of burnt clay, copper coins hammered out, and rudely engraved with hieroglyphics. The caskets are of sun-dried clay, and are covered with picture writing and hieroglyphics. The caskets seem to be intended as receptacles for the tablets of record. They have close fitting covers, which are cemented on with Assyrian like cement, and various figures were molded on the top, the ancient Sphinx, beasts, serpents, human faces with head dresses or crowns.

All around Michigan, including the surrounding states, many people were in the relic business. Many mounds were found and uncovered. It seemed that when one mound was found several more were found in the immediate area. The relics in the mounds caught the interest of Daniel E. Soper, a former Secretary of State, and a respectable businessman. He combined his efforts with the Reverend James Savage and together they made more important discoveries. Savage stated:

We have opened more than 500 of these mounds in the four counties in which we have worked, a territory exceeding over 260 miles. We have diligently inquired regarding the locality of other finds and have so far located sixteen counties in Michigan in which these specimens have been found. We are confident that we are only on the border land of the great prehistoric people.

Some of the people who dug the mounds came away very disappointed because a vast majority of them were without any relics or graves. They seemed to be just a big mound of earth. In spite of this, many thousands of relics were found, including remains of the ancient people who may have built these mounds. Many people were aware of the artifacts being uncovered and many articles were written about them. Daniel Soper reported to one newspaper. saying:

I have personal knowledge of more than 3,000 articles that have been found and if they are fakes and were buried to be found, whoever buried them has been a very busy person, because they have been found throughout the state by hundreds of different people. The objects recovered from the mounds are, variously, of copper, sandstone, limestone, burned clay and slate. The copper and slate objects predominate. The copper appears to be true mass lake copper. Of the slates the grayish black variety predominates, this being of the quality which outcrops near Baraga, in northern Michigan. The sandstone is of fine textured stone, now quarried at Amherst, in Ohio. Red and green slate limestone appear. These being of an argillaceous character and having a good polish.

Elder Bird and Elder Roundy were not the first Mormons to see the tablets, nor was Elder Milton R. Hunter the first LDS church authority to ever lay eyes on the famous collection. After the Smithsonian-Powell had entrenched in the minds of the scientific community that the tablets were a fraud, and at the height of the debate, Elder James E. Talmage of the LDS Council of the Twelve Apostles went to the city to spend some time with the Soper/Savage team. He spent a great deal of time interviewing people and even went as far as to do some excavations himself. He had watched others dig in mounds and then dug with his own team uncovering at least ten mounds, finding nothing. He, too, would write a scarlet letter calling the discovery a fraud. He gave his reasons in an interview with the *Deseret News* of Salt Lake City on August 5, 1911. Nobody questioned his findings because he was the authority on all doctrinal questions. This report angered James Savage to the point that he began to blast the Church of Jesus Christ of Latter-day Saints and their ability to tell the difference between what was fraud and what was authentic.

Today, the tablets lay quiet in the vaults of the Church of Jesus Christ of Latter-day Saints in downtown Salt Lake City, Utah. The crates stand silent and the contents remain covered. Only a privileged few have ever been allowed to view the collection and as far as this writer knows no one has studied the tablets since Milton R. Hunter passed away.

The following photographs depict such events as The Creation, the Flood, the Tower of Babel, the Birth of Christ, the Crucifixion, Mass execution by beheading, drowning, burning at the stake and more. The writings on the tablets are astounding. I could not show all the photographs but have elected to show the ones that I feel are most important.

The tablet above depicts the creation. This symbol, **⟘⧺⟩**, appears on all of the tablets including arrow and spear points. It may mean; "Deity."

The bottom tablet depicts the crucifixion.

What is thought to be the Ten Commandments.

Made from black slate, this tablet shows water torture, or death by drowning.

The Tower of Babel

This tablet depiction appears to be the handing down of the Ten Commandments.

Ancient writings that almost appear to be oriental adorn the tablet.

This tablets shows that there were Indians who traded with people who resembled Egyptians. It appears that they also battled with men that appeared to be Egyptian. There are a few characters that resemble Middle Egyptian grammar.

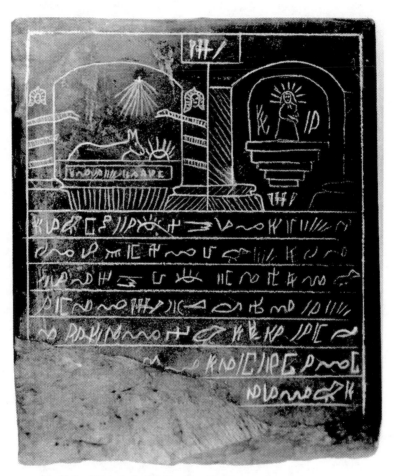

The birth of Christ is depicted on this tablet. Note the Egyptian characters.

This tablet shows a different type of script. The same "Deity" symbol appears on all tablets. This depicts the crucifixion of Christ.

Above appears a scene depicting the great flood.

A scene of a great mass execution by beheading

A beautifully etched black slate stone box hinged with pieces of gold straps.

CHAPTER 5
THE PADILLA PLATES

In March of 1961, two missionaries from the Church of Jesus Christ of Latter-day Saints by the names of Richard L. Averett and Gerald Kammerman happened to knock on the door of Dr. Jesus Padilla, a respected physician. This family was a wealthy one and was well known and liked throughout their community. The two missionaries had been assigned to the village of Cuautla, Mexico where the Padilla family had made their home. They were greeted by Mrs. Padilla who invited the two young men into her home so they could deliver their message. As customary, after the formalities were over, the missionaries handed the Padillas a copy of the pamphlet entitled *El Libro de Mormon: La Historia de las Americas Antes de Colon.* Dr. Padilla thumbed through the pamphlet until he came upon page five where he stopped and stared at the picture at the bottom of the page that had an artist's rendition of the gold plates uncovered by the prophet Joseph Smith. The drawing was of the plates stacked and bound with three gold rings. Also on that page was a copy of the Anthon transcript. Elder Averett later stated that, "While thumbing through the tract Dr. Padilla saw the characters of the Anthon transcript and exclaimed that he believed what the missionaries were telling him because he had discovered in a pre-Columbian tomb a set of gold plates with similar writing. He then showed us the three small gold phylacteries with the small hinges that Mrs. Padilla wore at her wrist. Each was inscribed with twenty five characters not unlike the characters on the tract. A small hinge was on the plates at the time and the remains of red fingernail polish was also visible."

After the missionaries left the Padilla home they reported what they had seen to their mission president, Harvey Taylor. President Taylor told Elder Marion G. Romney of the Counsel of the Twelve, who was visiting Mexico on other business. Elder Romney made an appointment to see the two young missionaries and to recommend that they submit the facts to Brigham Young University for evaluation. The two young men did as they were instructed and even submitted a photograph of the plates that Dr. Padilla had given to them. The picture was eventually given to Dr. Harold Christensen of the Archaeology Department at Brigham Young University. After some time had passed, Dr. Christensen sent a letter back to Elder Averett and told him that the plates were most likely fraudulent. He gave no reason why or how he came to that conclusion. Averett later stated that to his knowledge and belief he was the first missionary to have contacted Dr. Padilla. He further stated that he believed that Dr. Padilla did not know anything of the LDS church or the Joseph Smith story prior to Averett's first visit while tracking in that neighborhood.

Dr. Padilla would later comment that, "I knew nothing of the church until these two young men rang my door bell in 1961. The Elders saw the plates on display in a case in my living room and on my wife's wrist, and that is when they told me of the similarity of the characters."

The very existence of a set of gold plates with Anthon-type writing on them was more than enough to convince Jose Octavia Davila, a tour guide in Mexico, that something good might be in the wings. Davila was not without experience and expertise. He was an archaeologist in his own right and had accompanied Elder Milton R. Hunter on an expedition to the Lacandon Indian area in Southern Mexico and in Guatemala. He was involved with a team of BYU archaeologists who surveyed several Mayan areas during the mid to late 1950s. Davila assisted Dr. Wells Jakeman in the excavation of Izapa, Mexico, and had spent a great deal of time working with the New World Foundation.

Davila left as soon as he could for Cuautla to visit Dr. Padilla and view the gold plates for himself. He was greatly impressed by the characters on the five plates. He told Dr. Padilla that he believed them to be authentic and wanted to buy them for further study, but was stunned at the high asking price. Padilla, up until the great interest in his plates, thought that they were nothing more than jewelry for his wife. He hadn't placed high value on them, but now that they were on the minds of everyone he figured that they must be of some value.

Several months later, Davila had a surprise visit from Mrs. Padilla. She came to Davila's home in Pueblo, Mexico, to see if he was still interested in purchasing the plates. Davila found out the Padillas were in financial difficulties and needed money right away. Very excited, Davila negotiated for the plates and ended up buying them for two thousand dollars. He now had the plates. Later Dr. Padilla would state that there were no financial difficulties, that the money was paid for the purpose of lending them to Davila for study, and the plates were to be returned to him.

Not too long after, Jose Davila went on a mission for the LDS church in his Mexican homeland. His American wife went back home to Salt Lake City, Utah while her husband worked as a missionary. Davila told his wife to get an interview with the First Presidency and tell them of the plates. Hazel Davila was successful in getting an interview with the First

Presidency which then consisted of Presidents David O. McKay, Hugh B. Brown, and Henry Moyle. She offered the plates to the church as a gift but the First Presidency declined the offer suggesting, "While they may be of great value and importance, we have no way of displaying them, interpreting them, or evaluating their authenticity." The First Presidency suggested that the Davila's keep the plates and admonished Mrs. Davila to take great care of them. Mrs. Davila did not stop there. She finally got them into the hands of Milton R. Hunter who gave them to the Department of Archeology at Brigham Young University so that they could study and evaluate the plates.

The question came up as to how Dr. Padilla found these plates. Mrs. Davila wrote a letter to her husband and had him write back and tell the university what Padilla had told him concerning the origin of the plates. It was not known if he sent the information that his wife requested, but from other reliable sources the story is told that in the early spring of 1956, a group of treasure hunters were working a remote area in Mexico. They were looking for a stash of Spanish gold coins that a farmer had told them were hidden in a field that he owned. After the group had agreed to keep him in as a full partner, he showed them the field and the search was on. The leader of this group was none other than Dr. Jesus Padilla. All of the members of this treasure team were men of wealth and culture. They formed their group for weekend and holiday excursions. They were mostly interested in the ancient Indians of Mexico's past, but were not beneath a search for Spanish gold either. As these men were busy digging in the furrows of the farmer's field, a storm broke out over them causing them to dash for the safety of their tents. The storm continued into the night, and then a fierce wind began to blow which blew Padilla's tent so hard that one of the tent pegs came out of the ground. Padilla took a hammer and began to drive the peg back into the ground to secure the tent. As he was pounding the peg, the ground suddenly caved in and he dropped into a shallow chamber. He cried out for help and to his rescue came the rest of the group. They helped him out of the hole and into another tent for the remainder of the night.

When morning came, Padilla and the others examined the hole that he had fallen into. They removed the downed tent and began to excavate the hole. The hole quickly opened up and soon the group found that they were standing in the entrance of a tomb of sorts. They excavated more and found bones lying in a mixed order. They noticed that the tomb had been airtight until they had opened it. With flashlights in hand, they moved into the depths of the chamber looking at the walls, and soon they were surprised by strange writings on an opposite wall. The characters that they beheld were nothing like any of them had ever seen before. They were totally unknown and unfamiliar to any of the men.

Soon they came upon the center of the tomb. It was filled with stone plates and jars that appeared to be wrapped in some sort of paper. There was another body in the center of the room. Padilla examined the remains and found a number of small gold phylacteries. Three with hinges were attached to the wrist that lay across the collapsed chest. Two lay under the skull and three were upon the forehead. Four lay where the chest should have been and had been placed in a clay dish. The dish disintegrated when touched leaving the small gold plates intact. All were inscribed with strange characters similar to those on the tomb walls.

Padilla laid claim to the gold charms and a stone which had inscriptions. He kept a stela with the same type of writing on it. One of the group kept a stone sphere with the curious writing inscribed on both sides. The rest of the team took what pottery they could so they could sell it on the black market in Mexico City. When Padilla returned home he gave the gold plates to his wife. At the time he did not know that they were made of gold.

Soon after the Archeology department examined the plates, an article appeared in a *Newsletter and Proceedings of the Society for Early Historical Archaeology*. It was edited by a member of the Archeology Department quoting both Dr. Ross Christensen and Dr. Wells Jakeman as declaring the plates a fraud. The article pointed an ugly finger at the finder. In the critic's final paragraph, he reversed his position for fraud and suggested that should the plates prove to be authentic, a crime against the antiquities law of Mexico had been committed and that the subsequent sale and exportation from Mexico of the artifacts was illegal.

When Davila heard of this article he was very upset. He had returned from his mission and had set up residence in Utah. He retrieved the plates and continued to show them to his friends and remained a firm believer in their authenticity. He considered the criticism by the university authorities as frivolous.

In 1965, Davila sought help from Church Historian, Elder Joseph Fielding Smith. Smith gave Davila a copy of a manuscript entitled *Grammar and Alphabet of the Egyptian Language*. It was an unpublished work from the Kirkland, Ohio, *School of the Prophets* in which many of the brethren who attended were taught methods of Egyptian character translation by the Prophet Joseph Smith. Davila began to study and learn all that he could and discovered that many of the characters were exactly the same as the characters that were on the Facsimile #2 of the Pearl of Great Price. He was very excited with this discovery. He next began to research the correlation between the Anthon transcript, the Facsimile #2 of the Pearl of Great Price, and the work of the Egyptian grammar given him by the LDS church. He was more than convinced that the writings all came from the same language root.

Davila spent the next several years trying to translate the characters on the plates. It was during this time that a man by the name of Del Allgood from Fillmore, Utah gave him a call. Allgood had heard that Davila was learned in the translation of ancient writings and thought that he could be of some service to him. Allgood had found a rock in Chalk Creek Canyon, east of the town of Fillmore, that had strange characters on it. Allgood talked Davila into going with him into the canyon for further investigation of the characters. As it turned out, this act brought many problems to Davila, including ridicule because of the tragic deaths of two young men at the Chalk Creek site. This brought agony to Davila and embarrassment to the LDS Church, so in the year of 1970, Davila and his family returned to Mexico. A disillusioned individual, he had, in his own opinion, been greatly misunderstood by his Utah critics. He once again became a tour guide in Mexico.

The late Dr. Paul Cheesman heard about the Padilla plates through one of his students while lecturing at Brigham Young University. The student had met and become friends with Padilla while he was in Mexico. Cheesman had, for some time, compiled files on ancient writings. He was very interested in learning more about the man in Mexico who had in his possession plates with hieroglyphic writings on them. Cheesman soon arranged a meeting with Dr. Padilla at his home in Cuautla, Mexico. He was accompanied by Dr. Ray Matheny of the BYU Archaeology Department. Neither man had any previous knowledge of the Padilla-Davila connection. In an interview with Ray Matheny the following was related:

In January 1971, Dr. Padilla displayed for Dr. Paul Cheesman and me some of the plates and other artifacts reportedly taken from the Guerrero tomb. These consisted of numerous small objects including an array of jade beads shaped like calabashes, short tubes, and round forms, all drilled for stringing. Also found were carved shells, stone receptacles, carved obsidian and jade earspools, jade labrets (ornaments worn in perforation in the lip), monochrome pottery with cascabel supports (slit-type, bell like openings), projectile points, miniature pottery vessels, all of which appeared to be of a late date for Meso-America. The assemblage in general is of the Post Classic Period and strongly supports Padilla's claim that the material was taken from a tomb in Guerrero. The only objects conspicuously different from those normally found in tombs in the area are the gold plates.

The plates were photographed, and one of the small plates was given to Dr. Cheesman for the purpose of examination and authentication. The following September, Dr. Cheesman delivered a paper at the annual symposium of the S. E. H. A. held at BYU:

These twelve metal plates found by Dr. Padilla range in size from the largest, which is 5³/₈ inches long and ¹⁵/₁₆ inches wide, to the smallest which is ¹⁵/₁₆ inches long and ⁷/₁₆ inches wide. All were engraven on both sides.

One of these plates was brought to the United States for examination. A neutron analysis was made by the University of Michigan from two samples of the plate. The results revealed the composition of the metal to be 80.3% gold, 9.4% silver, and 10.3% copper. A density check confirmed the analysis. Of the twelve plates, seven are still in the possession of the finder. Photographs of the plate under magnification reveal that the engraving was made with a sharp metal tool that had a cutting point. The beginning and ending of each stroke was tapered. Max Weaver, an expert engraver with many years of experience, has analyzed these magnified photographs and has confirmed the above findings. The type of tool used was of hardened metal and could have been copper, bronze, or steel. An opinion has been expressed by all who have examined the photographs and the plates that whoever engraved them was an artful and experienced engraver. It is not likely that any electrical device was used to make the groves since that method would produce pulsating strokes.

The plate had been shown to Dr. Frederick Docstader, of the Museum of the American Indian in New York City, and to Dr. Gordon Ekholm, of the American Museum of Natural History in the same city. A third expert, Dr. Cyrus Gordon of Brandeis University in Waltham, Massachusetts, was also shown the plate. Only one of these experts would express a positive view that the symbols and the plate could very well be the old world influence of language and thus could be genuine. Dr. Cyrus Gordon insisted that he be allowed to meet and visit with the finder of the plate, which he was granted. He spent some time with Dr. Padilla and examined the plates very thoroughly, photographing them and making molds.

As time passed, Jose Davila met an old friend, and former business partner, Hector Huerta. Huerta told Davila that three men from the States had been visiting with Dr. Padilla concerning the plates. He had their names—Cheesman, Matheny, and Nibley. He told him that Padilla had shown them seven similar plates previously unknown to Davila. This was good news to Davila. He would make arrangements to study the inscriptions on them also. He once again headed for the city of Cuautla and the home of Dr. Padilla. Padilla did not want to see Davila and told him that he had to come back another time if he wanted to see the plates, and this time make an appointment. Davila made the appointment and returned to the home of Dr. Padilla only to be told that the LDS Church came and took the plates for study. This disappointed Davila very much. He decided that he was being put off by Padilla and that he had the plates, but for some reason, he didn't want Davila to see them.

In January of 1972, Davila met an old friend on the streets of Pueblo, Mexico. Kurt Olson, who was an old Brigham Young University associate, mentioned to Davila that he had heard Dr. Paul Cheesman was in Mexico to buy the Padilla plates. Davila was upset and shocked. He immediately left for Mexico City to visit with his long-time friend Hector Huerta. Huerta also heard of the visit to Padilla by Cheesman and told Davila that Dr. Padilla was asking thirty-five thousand dollars for the seven plates. This enraged Davila and he was determined to stop the sale. He was not mad at Cheesman but at Brigham Young University for offending him years ago. He made a beeline to the authorities and told them that he was aware of an illegal attempt to sell archaeological artifacts by Dr. Padilla in Cuautla. The weekend was upon them and Friday was a holiday, so the office would be closed on Saturday and Sunday. It wouldn't be until Monday before the authorities would act. Davila decided to call Padilla on the phone to tell him what he had done. Padilla was greatly outraged. He revealed to Padilla that he had registered all twelve plates with the National Museum of Anthropology, in his own name—a requirement under the law for privately held artifacts. He had barely accomplished this act within the time granted by a national antiquity amnesty. He then suggested to Padilla that he do something to protect his valuable collection from government confiscation.

Padilla didn't waste any time. He moved to dispose of his important artifacts in a judicious manner. He, too, reasoned that the authorities would visit him the following morning, which as expected, they did. He was pushed and shoved at gun point from his office at the National Social Security building, to his home, which had already been surrounded by soldiers. His wife was nearly hysterical when he arrived.

Padilla surrendered a few relatively unimportant artifacts and then explained that the rest of his collection had been stolen in a series of robberies reported to the police in months past. His story was confirmed at the police station where the records showed that he had reported a number of robberies at his home. The officials then went to the office of the local Mayor, who gave Dr. Padilla an excellent character reference. A call was placed to a high authority at the National Museum of Anthropology in Mexico City who confirmed that Dr. Padilla was the adopted son of Alfonso Caso, a renowned archaeologist. The authorities then stated, "It appears we have made a mistake, we have been misinformed."

Now the tide was about to change. Having successfully put off his own arrest, Dr. Padilla suggested to the police that the man they really wanted was Davila. Within three days the police entered the home of Davila seeking unregistered archaeological artifacts. Davila was not at home when they came, but his wife was. She produced papers showing registration under the procedures of the act of amnesty when they found a huge Mayan "Stela" in the courtyard. A number of security cameras that Davila had brought across the border on one of his trips to America were found. But again his wife presented the appropriate border papers proving registration of these items to the police. Not totally convinced, the captain ordered the confiscation of the cameras and charged Davila with possession of contraband. The captain had found a loop-hole in the law to arrest Davila. Davila had not returned to the border every six months to re-register two automobiles the police had found in his back yard. A warrant was issued for his arrest.

Davila was, at the time, an owner of one hundred acres of land bordering the archaeological zone at the ruin of Palenque in Chiapas, Mexico. Mrs. Davila drove through the night to reach her husband and tell him the bad news. The police had followed Mrs. Davila, and while she was in the camp talking with her husband, the police arrested him. He was charged at the scene with destruction of an archaeological zone because he had cleared an area for overnight camping sites. Davila was taken to jail and then transferred to the Lucumbre Federal Prison in Mexico City. This was to be his home for the next four years while he awaited trial to satisfy the slow process of the Mexican law which had indeed backfired on the unlucky man.

It wasn't long before two men from the United States paid Jose Davila a visit at the prison. These two men, whose names must remain anonymous, were after the golden plates for preservation. They are men with integrity and without guile. After they had gained Davila's trust, they planned their next move. Davila had explained that the little gold phylacteries were in a small box in the bottom of a container of sugar in the kitchen at his home. (Davila had five of the plates while Padilla had seven).

The two men found the home of Davila boarded up and sealed with an official seal. Each window of the home had been nailed shut and boarded up. These people really meant business. The men had made arrangements to meet with Davila's daughter, Laurie, for the purpose of getting to the plates. Laurie gave them the name of the next-door neighbor and then parked her car three blocks from the house. She elected to remain in the car until the mission was completed. The men entered a neighbor's gate, knocked on the front door and found the neighbors at home. They spoke English sufficient to communicate. They explained that they were friends of the Davila family and had come to see if they could retrieve some books for Jose from inside his home. They explained that Jose had told them that they could be trusted. The neighbors opened the front shades of their home and pointed to a window on the second floor of the apartment building across the street. They explained that a government man was at the window day and night. The lights were on and the shades open, but no one was watching from the window. It was suggested they wait until the lights went out.

After an hour or so the two men decided they could wait no longer. Laurie was probably beside herself with worry waiting in the car. They had to move quickly. The light had not gone out nor had they seen anyone in the window. "Operation Gold Retrieve" was about to begin.

The two men, who we will call Jake and David, suggested to the neighbor that they leave the villa and visit a friend. They left after turning out all of the house lights. Jake and David walked to the back door and crept into the side yard. The wall was higher than they had supposed. David handed Jake the rope and motioned for him to stand facing the wall. As Jake stood there, David stooped and boosted Jake to the top of the wall. Jake tumbled over the wall, secured the rope on the limb of a tree, and then threw the rope back to David. A moment later he was at Jake's side breathing heavily. Slowly they made their way through the shrubbery towards the front door. The light remained in the distant apartment but still no one appeared to be watching. They took a crowbar from the sack David had requisitioned from the neighbor, forced the door, and disappeared into the darkness of the home. David removed from his pack a pen light and began to search the kitchen. The sugar can was exactly in the place that Jose had described. Jake took off his glove, reached in and found a small jewelry box resting at the bottom of the sugar. He opened it and there were the five small golden plates nestled inside.

They moved to a bedroom filled with books and papers. David held the light while Jake rummaged through the collection. It seemed like it took forever to locate all of the papers and books Jose had requested. The gloves were a nuisance but they could not afford to leave any fingerprints behind. In their hurry, they could not find the first edition of the Book of Mormon that Jose had requested they retrieve.

David now had a sack full of books and papers and turned off the pen light as they stumbled through the dark to the front door. They cracked the door open slightly to view the window in the upper apartment across the street. The light was off. Jake was terrified. Had the agent seen them? The two men made a mad dash for the wall. David literally threw Jake to the top of the wall. Jake tumbled over and collapsed in a heap on the other side. He then recovered, got to his feet and out of the way as David came crashing down off the wall. David was a big man, and the earth shook as his large frame hit the dirt next to Jake. He knelt and asked if everything was all right with Jake. He replied that no bones were broken. They then crawled in the dark to the front gate of the neighbor's yard. They had not returned and the house was still dark. There were no signs of government agents. They opened the gate, slid through and walked briskly down the street. They dared not look back at the window across the street, nor was there a word spoken between them. As they rounded the corner they both broke into a dead run until they were in the back seat of Laurie's car. She was by then almost hysterical. She had imagined every possible problem in what had seemed like hours of waiting.

But there were two more obstacles before "Operation Gold Plate Retrieve" would be completed. The customs official stood waiting at the exit gate at the Mexico City Airport. Did he know? Jake patted at his toupee under which he had attached the five small golden metal plates. If caught, he would find himself a cell mate of Jose Davila. No one would suspect, he told himself, and walked through the gate with his bags in hand. David crowded with his luggage. The official looked past him to the blond girl in line. As they boarded the plane, Jake smiled at David. Los Angeles was only a few hours away.

The immigration official at the Los Angeles airport was formidable. He towered over Jake and asked, "Are you a citizen of the United States? How long have you been out of the country? What was the purpose of your visit abroad?" They answered his questions, trying to appear unworried. He looked through their bags, hesitated and then passed them through. Jake looked at David and tapped his toupee. David looked quickly back at the immigration official and then pushed Jake through the gate towards the exit.

The twelve golden plates are now in the private collections of two men who live in Utah. I have had the privilege of viewing and handling these priceless artifacts. It is a shame that they are still labeled as fraud by some of our most learned archaeologists. But as stated before, there are about as many others who will claim that they are authentic.

ANTHON SCRIPT

Jose Davila translated the Padilla Plates and sent the results to several individuals. The following is the Jose Davila translation:

To all those who have ears, listen! The anointed God, METCH, speaks. His words are as fire, with power to mold and perfect those who heed. He is the anointed one, the God of the celestial boat, who speaks Holy Scriptures. He teaches the correct way of life, that will bring brilliance and enlightenment to those who heed. Such ones will be beautified in Heaven. His words are of such power, that they reach to the depth of the underground sanctuary of the other world.

Mankind are sons of God, but have become corrupt and filthy. To those the Holy One speaks, that they might learn the correct way of life. He does not destroy them, but goes among them as a shepherd preparing to rise from the waters and from the earth. The holy ones, who are righteous, he will bring forth with a body of flame and fire. The wicked who reject his word will remain in their graves, in the underground chambers of the other world, cared for by the ancient earth god SEKER.

This Sky God, who loves mankind, descended from the sun to be born on earth and live among men. He is the lord of creation, lord of truth and light, lord of justice and mercy. He descended to put in order the paths and roadways for man. From the celestial regions he descended to die, to give the living and the dead, truth and exaltation in the heavens.

You rise from your grave in the mountains, oh God of the spirit, you who never knew corruption, you have defeated death, to be exalted as lord of justice and righteousness. You sit in glory on your throne. You are the judge who weighs on the scales and measures man's actions. You select and settle accounts. Some you reject and cast out. To the worthy you allot estates and bestow crowns of glory.

Oh God of justice, your sacrifice is for all mankind. You have opened up the graves of the dead. These shall be lifted up to be judged of you in holiness. You have broken the earth and kept open the doorway, that all may rise, because of your free offering. We sing praises and give honor bowed down with gratitude for this great gift. Mankind could not regenerate themselves, they had no power to do so, but the lord of creation, opened the door for regeneration and all will be raised at one time or another. They will be as numerous as the stars in the heavens. This God whose celestial boat was wrecked upon the cross, bestows a gift for righteousness. This gift is a divine body, like that of the first born.

There will be a time when the bodies of the dead will rest in their graves, but not all will have a peaceful wait. There are two places wherein the spirits dwell awaiting regeneration. Some souls are in anguish, others enjoy a state of rest. Since there is opposition in all things the force of evil has been present in man from the beginning.

There must needs be a place for these two opposing conditions, good and evil, one is called heaven, the other METNAL or hell. Nevertheless, those prisoners in hell are being taught the correct way of life and truth. They are being prepared for regeneration. A plan is being presented for their acceptance or rejection.

The three Gods [in] heaven, earth and the spirit world, descended through the under world, to teach, mold and prepare the dead for a return to life. These Gods have power to open the mouths of the dead and give them life again. Those who remain impure, will be judged, by the god who descended from the sun. He will pass righteous judgment upon the wicked. These souls will remain in METNAL. Those who have listened to the councils of the gods, will be given light and guidance. These are the harvest of the labors of god. Through their obedience they are reclaimed and led to the doorway.

The God of generation will receive as his seed this nation of foreign people, who were lost and found, through obedience. They have been formed and molded in the image and likeness of God. They will serve him and in time break out of the earth hastily, in a moment, as youthful Gods. Breaking the earth they hover light as air. Their figures are radiant. In a moment they are taken by the hand, by a group of gods, that help the dead and floating in the air as they approach the throne of God.

Those who have prayed and supplicated the Gods of heaven, will be received as their seed even as their children. They will be given a kind of garment pertaining to a divine body that will be eternal. These just ones are formed with the qualities of virtue, even the qualities of god. They will be crowned with power and authority for they have proved worthy to wield such power.

Those who are filthy and evil will be held back, in their graves, rejected by the just god, to remain for a time prisoners of the devil. They are as sleepers in their impurity and dishonor. They suffer humiliation and shame, in a state of helpless inactivity. One day they shall be brought before the tribunal to be judged. The judgment will be given according to the acts that have been recorded in the books, as has been commanded.

These wicked ones were and are slaves of the devil, chained to him by their own choice. They were free to choose. No one forced wickedness upon them. They are the thieves, liars, murderers, licecious ones and those who say one thing and mean another. These lost souls will await their judgment through a thousand years of peace, then they will stand their trial in court. The books will be opened, their acts will be weighed and measured, and justice will be done, by the God of truth and light. This God loved all men and would have had them as his seed, through obedience, but these rebellious ones were free to choose and they sought to serve the devil. Their misfortune will be to suffer a second death. They will be condemned to pass the time with the personified darkness, wailing their lot in pain and suffering, cast out forever into darkness beyond the sight of the divine group who were found worthy.

There will be great sadness over the loss of these wayward ones. No joy will be felt because of their fall. Where God dwells, they can never come, but great gladness will fill the courts because of those who were found worthy. These will have their healthy bodies renewed as shining temples. They will be crowned with glory. These are the virtuous ones formed in the image and likeness of God, persons of light and knowledge. These are glorious beings full of joy and happiness praising their God. These holy ones enter into the protecting gates of heaven, where all is peace and love. They are safe from all evil amid beauty and adornments beyond mortal description. Their mansions are allotted, according to their virture.

The sacrifice of the only begotten is fully realized in this highest glory. Those who inhabit it are counted as his children. They will multiply within their family. On the other hand the wicked will be confined without, guarded by a lake of fire. They will have no increase. Their splendor will be destroyed as an unopened bud is killed by the worm.

When the time has passed for mankind to work out his place in eternity, the one who controls, directs and supervises this earth's movements, will place a barrier of force to give peace to the world that it may rest from war and destruction for a thousand years. Some righteous ones will wait and remain to the last laboring. They will be lifted up high in greatness before the eyes as a group of gods. After the peaceful period, of a thousand years, the earth as it is now known, will come to an end. This orb will be transformed into an abode of beings of light. It will be changed by the visit of the great god who will grace it by his presence. This planet will glow and burn like a sun. It will have light in itself, to take its place in the celestial ocean. This was decreed and ordained by god from the beginning. At this time when Father visits this planet his posterity will be transformed into Gods, beings of light, wise and instructed fold, crowned in light as splendid youthful, Gods, men of righteousness, that adore truth and justice, clothed with virtue and character, in the likeness of God. These have the privilege of eternal increase, multiplying in the life to come. Theirs is the right to associate with the god in heaven. They can praise him for the things that exist. They will shout with joy and sing hymns of praise to the great God who changed the world into a lake of truth and flaming fire, for the benefit of his children.

This glorified earth will circle in its orbit as a shining sun. It will be a place of celestial flame and fire and the criptal scepter, a glorious temple of light, where the God of the soul and the first born will come to this earth. Baba will remain exalted as the God and ruler of this planet. Happy and fortunate will be those who overcome evil and choose the correct way of life, as was taught by the first born. These will be resplendent and beautiful souls—even as Gods. They will dwell in this glorified earth forever—co-creators of other planets—peopled by their spiritual offspring—continuing eternally creations in the universe.

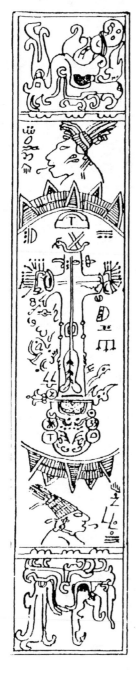
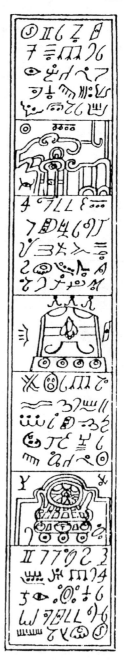

PLATE #1

PLATE #2

PLATE #3

PLATE #4

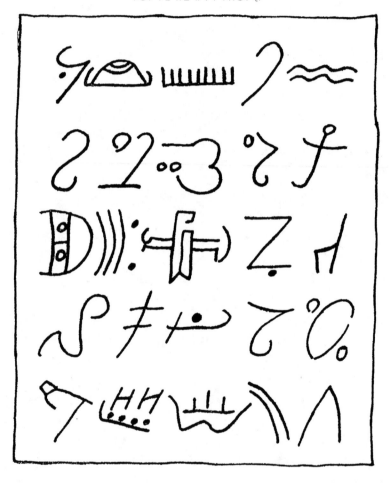

125

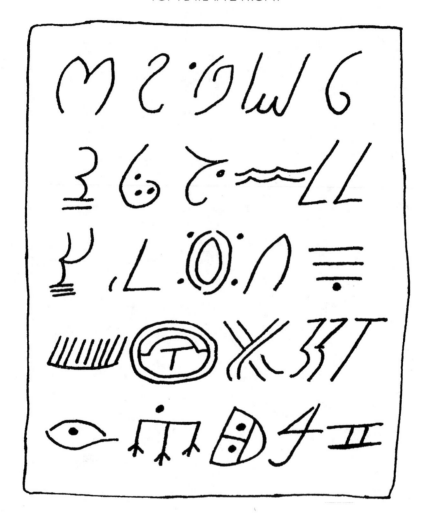

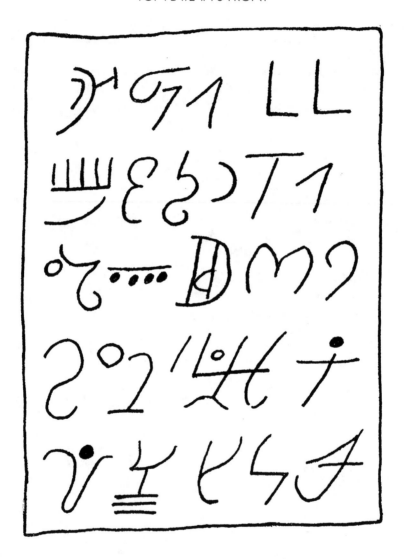

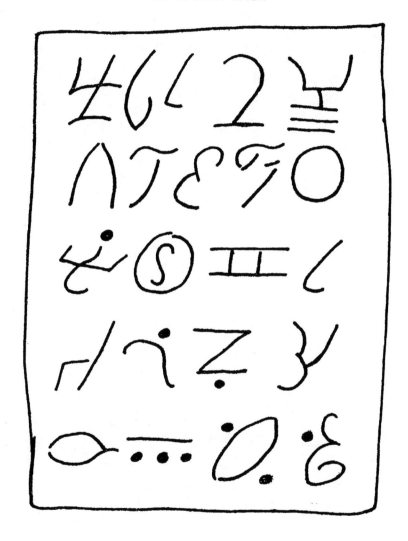

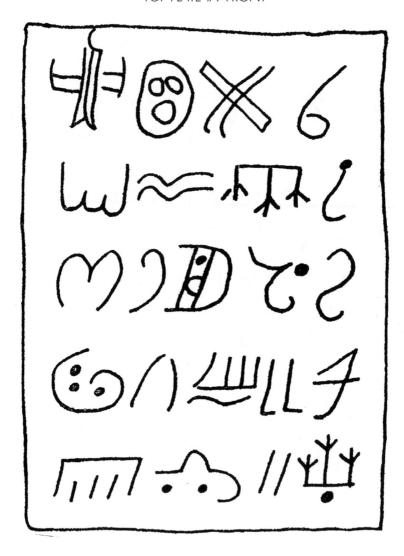

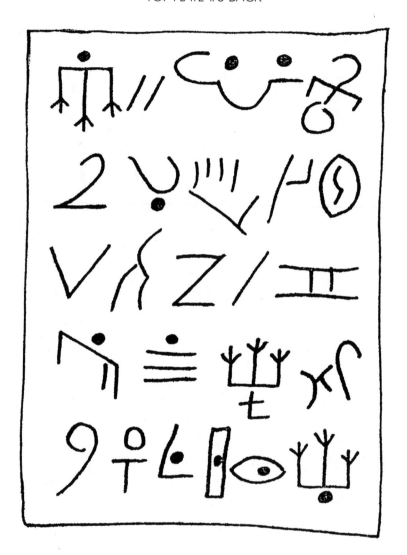

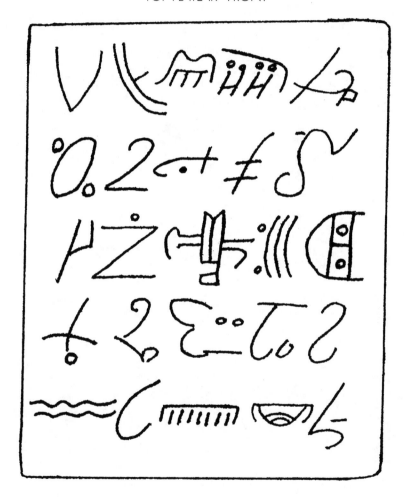

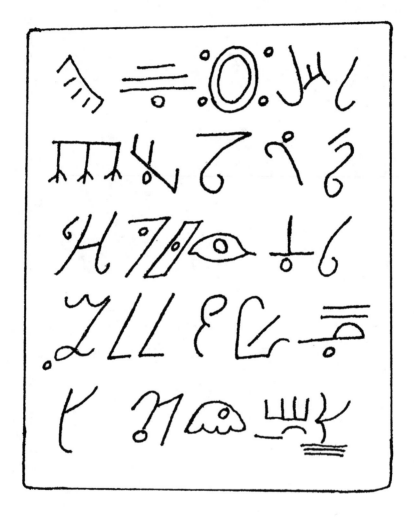

The following are pictures of the Padilla Plates and other artifacts found with them. The size of these small plates when seen next to the human hand, causes one to wonder at the artwork and craftsmanship detailed there. Whoever engraved these small golden plates was indeed a master of the art.

Notice how small the plates are.

Whether or not the Davila translation is true remains to be proven. The important thing here is that there were ancient plates found, and more importantly, they bear some of the same symbols as the Anthon Script as well as other writings found throughout the Americas.

The report by Paul Cheesman, Ray Matheny, and Bruce Louthan in January of 1973 concluded that they found the plates to have outward peculiarities which were not eliminated but increased by comparisons to other gold finds from Mexico and Central America. Chemical analysis was inconclusive, partly because of variation in the results; however, it seems likely that three sizes and at least two kinds of sheet gold stock were employed in the manufacture of the plates. Cheesman reported that in any case, the chemical analysis certainly did not provide clear substantiation for the antiquity of the plates since high percentages of gold (especially 70-80%) were rarely used outside of Colombia and Central America.

"Certain points remain to be made, however. It is possible that the plates were produced in two batches" contended Matheny. "No one saw the last seven, plates which Padilla still retains, until after October, 1961, when he gave the first five to Jose Davila. The differing chemical composition of the test samples from the two groups of plates may support this. Also, the first five plates were covered mostly with Anthon Transcript and other characters, while on the second seven, artwork generally predominates. Further testing of the engraving technique and composition through spectroscopic analysis could clear this up."

In conclusion, Dr. Matheny states: "The inescapable conclusion is that the Padilla gold plates are not artifacts of antiquity but of recent manufacture. The character analysis is conclusive demonstration that someone copied the Anthon characters from the Mexican mission tract without knowing that it was incomplete. The constituents of the plates, their uniformity of thickness, and surface finish further testify to a modern manufacturing technology. The art style of the plates is a complete anachronism in comparison to known ancient art of Meso-America, and most importantly, to the script."

It is very important that truth be sought after and that truth is always expressed. Throughout all ages there are some who have tried to deceive, thereby hiding the truth or bearing false witness. Until further evidence is brought forth, the scientific community will always contend that the Padilla Mexican plates cannot be considered authentic.

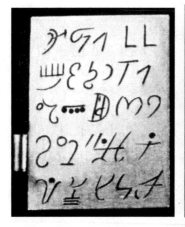

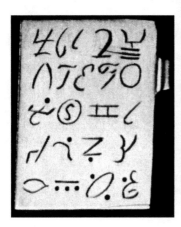

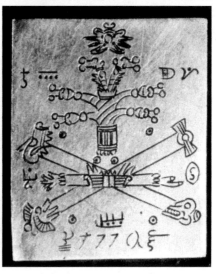

Notice the small hinges attached to each one of the tablets. When examined close-ly, it was almost impossible to see the weld. It took a master goldsmith to fasten these small hinges.

CHART OF CHARACTER COMPARISONS OF VARIOUS ANCIENT WRITINGS

Egyptian Heiratic J.S.Facsimiles Anthon Trans Padilla No.				Ecuador-Crespi Soper-Savage Kinderhook Manti W				Commentary
								No. system is digest of Padilla glyphs.[1]
01								
02								
03								
04								
05								
06								
07								
08								
09								
10								
11								
12								
13								
14								
15								
16								
17								
18								
19								
20								
21								
22								
23								
24								
25								
26								

CHART OF CHARACTER COMPARISONS OF VARIOUS ANCIENT WRITINGS

Egyptian Heiratic J.S.Facsimiles Anthon Trans Padilla No.				Ecuador-Crespi Soper-Savage Kinderhook Manti W					Commentary No. system is digest of Padilla glyphs.
27	(glyph)								
28	(glyph)								
29	(glyph)	(glyph)							
30	(glyph)	(glyph)	(glyph)				(glyph)		
31	(glyph)		(glyph)				(glyph)		
32	(glyph)						(glyph)		
33	(glyph)								
34	(glyph)			(glyph)	(glyph)		(glyph)		
35	W	(glyph)				W			
36	(glyph)			(glyph)			(glyph)		
37	(glyph)	(glyph)	(glyph)			(glyph)	(glyph)		
38	(glyph)					(glyph)			
39	(glyph)	(glyph)						(glyph)	
40	(glyph)		(glyph)						(glyph)
41	(glyph)	(glyph)							
42	(glyph)				(glyph)				
43	(glyph)								
44	(glyph)								
45	(glyph)								
46	(glyph)	(glyph)				P			
47	(glyph)	b							
48	(glyph)	(glyph)							
49	(glyph)								
50	(glyph)	(glyph)	(glyph)			q			
51	(glyph)	(glyph)							
52	(glyph)								

CHART OF CHARACTER COMPARISONS OF VARIOUS ANCIENT WRITINGS

Egyptian Heiratic J.S.Facsimiles Anthon Trans Padilla No.				Ecuador-Crespi Soper-Savage Kinderhook Manti			W	Commentary No. system is digest of Padilla glyphs.
53								
54								
55								
56								
57								
58								
59								
60								
61								
62								
63								
64								
65								
66								
67								
68								
69								
70								
71								
72								
73								
74								
75								
76								
77								
78								

CHART OF CHARACTER COMPARISONS OF VARIOUS ANCIENT WRITINGS

Egyptian Heiratic J.S.Facsimiles Anthon Trans Padilla No.				Ecuador-Crespi Soper-Savage Kinderhook Manti W					Commentary — No. system is digest of Padilla glyphs.
79	)		)			)			
80	ꝯ		ꝯ				ꝯ		
81	ꝯ°		ꝯ°	ꝯ°					
82	ꜿ		ꜿ						ꜿ
83	⌣̈		⌣						
84	)'								
85	⌂								
86	⋈								
87	-))	)₊	)	⟩		⫲			
88	))₊								
89	)))								
90	)((		)((						
91	°()	°()		()		⌒			
92	(λ		ʃ			⫶			
93	ꝏ		ꝏ			⫶			
94	ꝏ								
95	ꝏ		⌣						ꝏ
96	ꝏ	co	ꝏ			ꝏ			
97	ꝯ		ꝯ						
98	✓	✓	✓°						
99	✓	°ᴶ	ꝯᴶ	ᴶ	✓				
100	✓								
101	✓								
102	✗°								
103	⫲		⫲			⊢	⊏		
104	⫲								

CHAPTER 6
MYSTIC WRITINGS AND LOST TREASURES

Egypt has generally been considered to be the birthplace of writing. The ancient Egyptians did not write by letters as we do, but by signs expressing words, ideas, and concepts, This is referred to as hieroglyphic writing and *"is related to the principle of rebus or charade."*[1] It is sometimes referred to as idiogramic writing.

In ancient times the writing was accomplished in several ways. Copper, bronze, and iron chisels were used to inscribe the writing on stone and wood, while the reed was used to write inscriptions on rolls of papyrus using ink make from vegetable substances, or colored earth. Whatever the method, we are left with a great many inscriptions telling us of ancient Egyptian culture. *"It was the Egyptians who developed this science of symbolism and are looked upon as its real founders."*[2] However, some scholars believe that the Hebrew patriarchs may have originated the hieroglyphic. (Refer to first chapter.)

This was the language of the biblical patriarchs and was passed on down through Noah to his sons who inhabited the world after the flood. It was through Egyptus, the wife of Ham that Egypt was first settled, taking with them into the land a knowledge of the first writing taught to Adam.

"The land of Egypt being first discovered by a woman, who was the daughter of Ham. Now the first government of Egypt was established by Pharaoh, the eldest son of Egytus, the daughter of Ham, and it was after the manner of the government of Ham, which was patriarchal."[3]

If the first government of Egypt was established after the manner of the patriarchs then it is reasonable to believe that the reading and writing system was also borrowed from the patriarchs. *"It is hardly probable that the hieroglyphic system of writing was invented in Egypt, and the evidence on this point now accumulating indicates that it is brought from elsewhere."*[4]

According to Sir Alan Gardiner, a very well respected English Egyptologist, *"The Egyptian language is related to the Semitic tongues (Hebrew, Arabic, Aramaic, Babylonian). In general structure the similarity is very great,"*[5] This would help to explain why the hieroglyphic writing appears to have been in full bloom from the beginning without benefit of evolution. *" The sudden appearance of this well-developed form of writing (Egyptian hieroglyphs) indicates that it was most likely imported into Egypt from elsewhere. Some architectural features are similar to the earliest Mesopotamian civilizations and the rulers of Egypt and Mesopotamia had a common ancestry.*[6]

It is also very clear that from the Abraham writing in the Pearl of Great Price that they were written in hieroglyphics with a strange and unusual relationship to the Egyptian hieroglyphic. Facsimile #1, Facsimile #2, Facsimile #3, of the book are definitely related to the idiogramic writing that was the standard for the pharaohs. According to the Prophet Joseph Smith the papyri from which he took his translation was written by the hand of Abraham, and in the language of Abraham. Yet a well known professor at the Brigham Young University, an articulate student of Egyptology, and other well qualified Egyptologist are not able to translate the characters on the facsimiles to correspond with the writings in the Book of Abraham as published.

"The Hebrews have had wisdom of the Egyptian (writing) before Egypt herself did. Abraham, who lived with the priest of Heliopolis and taught them about the stars according to one ancient account, may well have taught them this too. The rich variety of the created world was a gallery of images or symbols for early man to puzzle out. All the things that Adam and Enoch saw were like letters illuminated by God. It was the Egyptians who developed this science of symbolism to the full extent."[7]

It is the conclusion of some as to the origin of the Egyptian hieroglyphic; that it was inspired by the original language and writings of the patriarchs beginning with Adam. it was brought into Egypt by the descendants of Ham and Egyptus and later fortified by Abraham. The original writing was later modified and changed into the hieroglyphs of the pharaohs, who lost much of the meaning of the various hieroglyphic symbols as known by Abraham and the patriarchs and corrupted them into symbols meaning that best represented their philosophy.

What about the strange writings on the rocks around areas like Fillmore, Nephi and Cedar City, Utah? They are similar to that of the Soper/Savage tablets and to the writings of Abraham. The stories that surround these figures on the rocks are never ending and always interesting. One such story includes our friend from a previous chapter, Jose Davila.

It was a very warm autumn afternoon in 1964 when Harry Fowler brought his 1956 Ford station wagon to a stop at a corner service station on main street in downtown Fillmore, Utah. The car was hot and steam blew out from under the hood. Del Allgood smiled to himself as he filled a water bucket from a hose that was coiled up at the side of his station. He was a rock hound and had to step over the many rocks to get to the hosebib. He had all sorts of polished and unpolished rocks, weathered and dead wood laid out in the car stalls. It didn't really look much like a service station at all. Fowler noticed all the rock and wood lying around and while Mr. Allgood was putting water into his car, Fowler noticed a piece of twisted cedar that seemed to stick out from the rest of the clutter. "Nice piece of wood; where did you get it?" he inquired. "Up Chalk Creek Canyon near the rock with the strange ancient writings," replied Allgood sticking his head out from under Fowler's hood.

The mere mention of the word "ancient" was enough to raise curiosity in Harry Fowler. He had just been a recent participant in an excursion to Mexico, Guatemala, and the Yucatan, with a tour guide of Indian descent who had spent a great deal of time talking about the ancient writings of his ancestors. Fowler had not paid much attention to the heat gauge on the station wagon because his mind was rehearsing the tour he had taken earlier that spring. Fowler then asked what kind of petroglyphs they were, to which Del Allgood replied, "Not anything like the usual hunting scenes of the Anazai. No sir, I never seen anything like them before." He went on to say that they seemed to resemble the writings of the Egyptians. Fowler then told Allgood that he knew of a man that could read the writings and then gave him the name of the native Huaztec-Mayan Mestize Indian from Mexico.

After Fowler had left, Allgood paused for only a minute and then dialed his friend Harold Huntsman to tell him of the interesting conversation he had with the passing motorist. "I think we ought to get hold of this guy in Salt Lake and see if he can tell us anything about these writings," he suggested.

Mr. Huntsman was in agreement and therefore a telephone call was made to Jose Davila. Davila was then living in Salt Lake working on the translation of the previous five golden plates that he had acquired from Dr. Padilla in Mexico. Allgood promised to reimburse his bus fare to Fillmore if he would come immediately and look at the writings. Davila consented and the next morning he took the early morning bus to Fillmore where he met Huntsman. He was driven to the symbol rock east of Fillmore in Chalk Creek Canyon. Davila was shown the rock with twenty-five unusual inscriptions. He immediately recognized a strange correlation with the characters on his gold plates. Some had similar strokes and connotations and a few were exact duplicate characters. He stood mesmerized; he could hardly believe his eyes. Two thousand miles removed was proof enough that his gold plates were for real.

Davila made copies of the symbols so that he could study them once back in Salt Lake. It was his first opinion that there was some Egyptian influence in this writing. Within a few days, Davila let Allgood know that he had translated a number of the signs and was "most excited over them. They talked of sacred records deposited at that location and gave instructions as how to retrieve them."

Allgood was patient with Davila as he struggled to decipher the characters. Finally with the help of other interested friends, Davila convinced Allgood that they should begin the work of discovery. Several people assisted him in the financial burden of road-building and site-preparation. Davila paid for 680 feet of core drilling in the hopes of discovering a hidden chamber or narrow the chances of locating the treasure. The year passed uneventfully and no treasure was found.

In August of 1966 while most of America's young men were going to war in Viet Nam, Davila and company were back on the site in another effort to find the chamber with the hidden records. The winter had been spent by Davila as a tour guide in Mexico and in his off time he had refined his measurements as to the location of the chamber. This year he planned on working hard and with a renewed vigor. Within two months, they had driven a hole in the hard rock to a depth of 80 feet. This shaft mushroomed at the bottom and had been forced with dynamite charges. It was their intention to drill exploratory holes in a 360 degree circumference. They would then set off dynamite charges to gain entrance into the chamber. According to the deciphered instructions on the rock it would be reached at 68 to 72 feet down, depending on the exact length of the ancient cubit.

In September, Davila was stricken with a ruptured appendix and was hospitalized. When he returned, he was of little help in the physical work taking place at the mine site. Two young men, who were returned missionaries of the LDS Church from respectable families, had volunteered to do some, if not most, of the work. Duane White and Kent Neely were both married with small children and were highly regarded by their friends and neighbors. They were very excited about the prospects of the hidden records.

About one-half mile up the hillside, a young California entrepreneur by the name of Devon Standfield was prospecting for gold in his own private endeavor. He, too, was digging a shaft on claims of his own. When his excavations discovered a narrow cavity in the hillside, he ingeniously pumped smoke into the mountain. It disappeared into the cavity. Stanfield scoured the hillsides for evidence of another outlet. No smoke reappeared regardless of how long he pumped. He concluded that the smoke was disappearing into a large underground chamber.

By now the townspeople were beginning to talk. Excitement filled the air as prospects of a strike appeared eminent. Standfield's mining claims had been filed all too close to the location where Davila and company were working. In an effort to ward off any difficulty, Del Allgood and Jose Davila filed placer claims over Harold Huntsman's lode claims to reinforce the situation. When Huntsman learned about this action, he became very angry. Perhaps he felt betrayed and left out. Regardless, he moved to eliminate the problem. On Saturday, November 5, 1966 he went out to the site of digging and ordered the two young men working in the shaft to leave the site. The two men told the angry owner that they were there working under Davila's approval, but Huntsman angrily assured them that he would return with the sheriff if they did not leave. The work stopped and the two men went home.

Davila immediately called the group together and made the decision to make an all-out effort to get into the chamber before the sheriff or anyone else made an appearance. They drilled three 20-foot holes west at the bottom of the shaft. They loaded the holes with ninety-one sticks of dynamite with 60% powder and lit the fuses. The blast rocked the mountain and the foothills surrounding them. It was Sunday, and most of Fillmore was observing the Sabbath, but this situation demanded that these LDS men work this day.

It was about 4:00 p.m. when the blast went off. Three air hoses from a compressor were then dropped into the dusty shaft and then the young men, who had been fasting this day, elected to go into town to enjoy their only meal of the day. A few hours later the men returned. Kent White was the first to go down and see if they had penetrated the hidden chamber. He had a happy look of expectation on his face as he descended the ladder. When he did not respond to inquiries made from above, Duane Neeley descended to see what the problem was. He, too, did not return. He, too, was overcome by the fumes that had not been cleared as a result of the blast. When he did not respond, his parents were summoned to the site. Mary Neeley headed back to town for help. The Sheriff deputies and firemen that arrived on the scene were unable to effect a rescue because of the noxious fumes. Hours later, Del Allgood recovered the lifeless bodies of the two young men. He telephoned Davila, who was recuperating from his operation, and he immediately drove to the site.

The Salt Lake Tribune published an article with the heading proclaiming death of the two young "Mormon Missionaries Searching for Gold Plates." The article devastated the parents of the two fine young men and placed the blame on Davila. It was a bitter ending to the Fillmore project. Any sympathy of the church hierarchy disappeared with the morning headlines. Davila found himself the subject of ridicule among former friends. The following day, Davila descended into the shaft with a gas mask to examine the effects of the blast. To his surprise, the dynamite had not penetrated the rock. He surmised that the blast had backfired without forward penetration. They had not broken into a chamber.

At the funeral of the two young men in Salt Lake City, Davila was informed that Huntsman had brought suit against him in a local court and the judge had issued a restraining order against him from further effort on the mine site. The Bureau of Mines closed the mine for an investigation.

In August of 1967, almost one year later, Devon Stanfield set off a dynamite charge in a tunnel on his claims. He, too, could not hold back his enthusiasm and went into the mine without proper ventilation. Fumes overcame him, and he, too, was a victim to Chalk Creek Canyon. When Davila and Huntsman finally made it to court Davila tried to prove that he had kept the claims valid from the work he had been doing, and that Huntsman had not done any assessment work at all. The outcome of the trial was that Huntsman was awarded $10,000 in damages. Davila ended up paying $500.00 to Harold Huntsman. According to Court records, Davila made the following statement to Huntsman:

> The object of my excavation is to reach into the hearts of man, and bring them unto God our Lord. I feel that I have not been sent to Fillmore to bring about the damnation eternally of anyone, but the interest is to bring out of their resting place the records that will bring millions of mankind into salvation and equalization.

It was also found out at the trial that Davila and Stanfield had became bitter enemies. Stanfield had told Davila to get off the property and never set foot back on it again. Court documents record the following:

> One evening Bill and Darlene Mundy and Verne and Luana Cluff rode up to the hieroglyphics to see how Jose was doing. As we approached the site from the south, we could hear some arguing going on. Jose and Stanfield were having words and were shouting at each other. Stanfield picked up a shovel that was lying there and raised it up to hit Jose over the head with it. Bill Mundy stepped in between them and grabbed the shovel. He showed Stanfield his Jeep Posse badge and told him he had the authority to arrest him if he continued fighting. Jose said Bill saved him from getting killed. Jose remarked one time that the first capitol of Utah being located at Fillmore, Utah was not a mistake and that some day Fillmore would be put back on the map.

The story of how the two young men died differs from the story Davila told according to Court records;

They set a charge of dynamite off in the hole and figuring they could never set foot on the land again, they went to town to get a hamburger while the gasses cleared out of the hole. They went back up on the site, and being anxious to see what the dynamite had uncovered, and thinking they could never come on the property again, we lowered Wilford White into the shaft in a bucket. When the line went limp, we pulled the bucket up and then we sent a second man, Kent Neeley down the shaft. He signaled for me to pull him back up. He was nearly to the top when the bucket went limp and I figured that he had been overcome by the gases and had fallen out of the bucket, down the shaft. I went for help in town. Both boys were killed. The shaft was 93 feet deep and Jose figured the treasure should be down about 110 feet.

The Petroglyphs, Judge, are a fine example of Nephite Reformed Egyptian Writing. My interpretation, that I could see had reached your hands also during this trial, stands against the learned scholars of the world as the Key to decipher this language. Naturally the Egyptologist will argue it to death; but if there was a key already deciphered to read Nephite Writing, the 7 lines and 233 characters of Anthon Transcript that Joseph (Smith) copied of plates and gave to Martin Harris to take to Professor Anthon in New York, would have been deciphered long ago; however no one has done that because there is no key. My translation puts the scholars in an embarrassing position for it merely points out that the Bibiteral and Triliteral Sense-idiograms that are used as complementary signs in Hieroglyphic, Hieratic or Demotic phonetical Egyptian Script are in fact the Original Egyptian Written Language, and that the later phonetical writing systems are but a reversion from this language and highly concentrated form of writing. Curiously enough this concise form was dropped in Egypt, but continued in America by Lehi's colony, with the texts of the Brass Plates that Laban had, and that the Egyptologist recognized such a concentrated language existed and have even deciphered numerous sense-ideograms; but have desisted from syntax-grammatical studies to define and further explore it. What I do in my translation is use the Egyptologists and translation of the Sense Signs, but I prefer to read them in the simplest form to me, that is under English Syntax, and that is what bothers the Egyptologists. These scholars do not seem to realize that if I were an ancient Egyptian I would read these sense signs with the Egyptian Syntax, of those days. But since these ideograms express full ideas, I am left to read them today in the best manner that will make sense to me, and that is in English Syntax. However in my study of the characters I do give the Egyptian Grammatical law that appears in the content and prove beyond a doubt that the text was written by some well versed scholar in ancient Egyptian. It will some day be accepted as the FIRST SUCCESSFUL INTERPRETATION OF NEPHITE WRITING.

My research of Nephite/Lamanite Civilization began in 1964 in Mexico. Since then I have been privileged to report of several archeological expeditions associated with the LDS Institution in the Maya Area.[8]

During an interview by Darlene Mundy with the author, she reported the following:

In 1964, I was told about the hieroglyphics up Chalk Creek Canyon in Fillmore, Utah. At that time Jose Davila and E. Del Allgood were digging a vertical shaft on the mining claim owned by Harold Huntsman.

It took Jose Davila three years to make a translation of the petroglyphics, and from his translation, mostly with the use of Budges Dictionary, he claimed the top character means: TO DIG OUT OF THE EARTH GARLANDED ETERNAL MINERAL RECORDS WHICH ARE HOUSED IN A NATURAL STONE CHAMBER. The other characters tell where the records are supposed to be.

Jose Davila says the petroglyphs are a fine example of Nephite Reformed Egyptian writing, which he had been studying for the last four years. Jose told me that in Cumorah, Ramah, Old Mexico, when the last battle took place between the Lamanites, Nephites and Jaredites, there were 24 Nephite survivors. Mormon and his son were among the survivors. The Book of Mormon says they took 24 tablets and fled. Jose Davila thinks these are the Golden Plates or metal tablets that are the sealed portion of the Golden

Plates, which according to LDS doctrine is yet to come forth. The same hieroglyphics are also in Cedar City and Manti, Utah.

Jose claims that the enemy was so close and the tablets were weighting them down, so that when they got to Fillmore the Nephites dropped Moroni off and went on to Manti, Utah. The last great battle took place and the 23 survivors perished. Moroni was spared as he was left in Fillmore. Moroni found ore and melted it (down) and translated the portion of the plates that he took to the Hill Cumorah and was later found by Joseph Smith. After Joseph Smith got through with them he was told to deposit them back in the Hill Cumorah. Jose Davila says Moroni retrieved them and brought the plates back to Fillmore and deposited them with the original ones, which is the sealed portion of the Book of Mormon that is yet to come forth. At this time he added ANGEL to his MORONI signature on the Petroglyphs. That is why his signature is not the same spacing between each letter as the other Petroglyphs. After that he went to New York or Hill Comorah and became ANGEL MORONI.[9]

The following is an interview with Clifford Purcell, from March 8, 1982. Tom Stinson, Bill Wright, and Darlene Mundy were present, and the following information was transcribed from a tape:

In 1939 I met Rube Melville who was running a little cafe in Fillmore, Utah, and he knew that I like to prospect. He told me there was some iron ore up the canyon. He told me there was some copper, and silver, as he had found a piece that indicated that there might be some there.

We went up Chalk Creek and went up on that ridge that goes up there, that hogs back, and I went with him and we got up the top and he went scouting around on the level as he was a heavy set fellow and it was hard for him, and I went further north and I turned and as I came down below the ledge and I was walking along there and I looked up and here was this writing on this rock. I looked at it and wondered why anyone would do anything up there. Away out of the way place, but I went on down, we were prospecting, and we found a little trickle or two of ore. Upon investigation it was proved there wasn't anything there. It was just a little dab of stuff. I asked Rube at the time, "What about that writing up there on that cliff?"

He said, "What writing?" I said, "Don't you know there is writing up there on that cliff? There is one that faces west and then there is a hand and a eye looking thing that faces to the north." He said, "I know about the map rock, there is a big rock down there that has a map drawn on it." He labored around with me kinda puffing and we went back up and took a look at it. He was astounded. Everything is so symmetric and perfect in writing. He didn't know anything about it and we came back to town. There are four rows kinda like picture writing full of lichen, full of green stuff. The sun was shinning on it. I went back up years later and found that some of it had fell down because of the rock freezing. I heard that it took a 1000 years to grow that depth of moss on the rocks. Chief Sobaquin said he did not know writing, it was long before his people. He thinks the map rock relates to the hieroglyphics. I think that the 3 dots line up and point to the hieroglyphics. The channels are under ground lines of gold that are set on the same tilt as the land.[10]

When Dr. Hugh Nibley, the articulate BYU Egyptologist, learned of the writings on the rocks at Fillmore, he knew of the involvement of Jose Davila, this celebrated Indian who claimed to translate reformed Egyptian. He chuckled to himself and after a cursory examination of the characters dismissed them as "Cowboy scratching." Had he realized how extensive these writings were throughout the western United States, he would have been forced to add that this same cowboy must have been mighty busy at that.

On June 5, 1988, Dr. Paul Cheesman and David Tomlinson presented a paper at the World Cultures of Ancient America Congress of the Epigraphic Society, held in San Francisco, California. This paper identified 14 sites including the Fillmore rock in which writings of the exact same nature are located. Subsequent to this presentation, five additional sites have been identified, making 19 sites located. Four of these sites are within a 35 mile radius of Berkeley, California. One is located near Dunsmuir, California, one near Lone Pine, California, and one in Genoa, Nevada. Still others are found at Nephi, Utah, which consists of two groups: Cedar City, Utah; Pocatello, Idaho; Ogden, Utah; Grand Junction, Colorado; Del Norte, California; Lake Powell, Utah; and Myton, Utah. According to Tomlinson, "They are generally located on a rock outcropping, often on or near a ridge line, usually prominent, with no apparent attempt to conceal nor reveal...One of the more prevailing influences in these glyphs is Egyptian. In addition to the widespread occurrence of the

'Ankh' or Egyptian 'life' symbol, the majority of glyphs bear some influence quickly recognizable as Egyptian."

On one of his trips back to the site of the Fillmore glyphs, Del Allgood discovered a section of lumber containing a message, which had been placed in a hole at the base of the rock containing the petroglyphs. The message, written in red ball-point pen upon the piece of wood stated, "To gold book your American finding here we are HMONG peoples. We goted already in Laos if need to know further information Welcome to Laos." On the same piece of wood were a group of twenty-two characters, twelve of which were among the twenty-five inscribed petroglyphs at either the Fillmore site or one of the other locations, and ten interspersed characters which were unknown. The whole of the characters was arranged in the same fashion as the rock petroglyphs. Allgood immediately contacted a Hmong friend who was working in Fillmore at a mushroom factory. He was told by his friend that the message was left by seven Hmong friends from California who had recently visited the man at the factory. While waiting for their friend to get off work, they drove into the nearby hills east of the city to enjoy the mountains. One of the Hmong visitors suddenly became excited when he saw the petroglyphs and said that he understood them, and therefore left the message on a board he picked up at the site. They returned to town and told their friend at the factory of their discovery. A few days later, they returned to California. Allgood pressed the man for more information as to the identity of the seven and the individual who left the message on the piece of wood. Unfortunately, before he was able to obtain this name, the worker at the factory moved to California himself.

David Tomlinson was so excited about the Fillmore story, he purchased the placer claims to the site. He contacted Del Allgood and an effort was made to contact the man who could reveal the identity of the writer on the piece of wood. After several years of correspondence, the trail had led only to some people near the Sacramento Valley who claimed they were relatives of the writer, but wanted to know more about the motives of Tomlinson and Allgood before they would reveal any further information as to the whereabouts of the man they were seeking. They did reveal that "Something gold of importance is buried at the site," but would not reveal anything further.

Tradition has it among the Hmong people that they originated near what is now England, and then migrated into Mongolia. They then settled in China, farming its river valleys for many centuries. Bullied by Hun invaders from the north, they renewed their southern migration. The Chinese called them barbarians but they have always referred to themselves as "Hmong," which means "free men." Although generally considered to be originally from China, they differ in as much as they are shorter and their eyes show less epicanthic fold or Mongolian slant.

In 800 B.C., the Chinese drove the Hmong into the mountains of Kweichow province. From there they settled also into what is now called southern Hunan, Tonking, Burma and Laos.

Linguistically they are far apart from the Chinese, and their language has not been established as being affiliated with any other known language. Their language has a special meaning as a symbol of ethnic identification for the Hmong, since theirs is essentially an oral tradition. They fear that the loss of their language would mean loss of their sacred traditions. They are bound by a belief of their being a "special people whose existence has a purpose for all mankind."

Hmong people have a tradition that the Chinese burned their ancient books and threatened death to anyone who continued writing in the old script. Some of the Hmong women used the old script alphabet as designs in their textiles and clothing, thereby preserving some of their script from the watchful eyes of the overlords. In spite of their endeavors, the ancient written language eventually became lost, except to be referred to in their oral traditions.

Dr. Paul Cheesman did a study relating to the Hmong people, and in a paper presented at the Epigraphic Society, he reported that earliest efforts to develop the Hmong oral language into a written alphabet appear in 1952, when Catholic and Protestant missionaries developed the Romanized Popular Alphabet for the Hmong oral language. A draft plan was presented in 1956. Others worked until 1982 when an English—Hmong Phrasebook With Useful Wordlist was developed by Cheu Thao at Washington, D.C, Center for Applied Linguistics. Finally, in 1983, that center developed a primer.

Interestingly however, the non-English message left at the Fillmore site by Hmongs was not written in the Romanized Hmong language, rather, it was written in what has become known as "Pahawh Hmong," a language purported to be the ancient lost language of the Hmong ancestors, which was restored to the Hmong by supernatural means in the 1950s.

It is said that a Hmong farmer named Ntxoov Zuha had twin sons who died, and subsequently appeared to him in a dream, indicating that they were to teach him the lost ancient Hmong language. He protested that he could not learn the language, but his sons convinced him to try. Over a period of two months, he was visited nightly in dreams until he had mastered the system of writing. He then published the system and taught some of the Hmong in Laos the language, but his followers were scattered and killed, and then he was killed in 1967 by Communist aggressors. Since that time the Hmong have been very secretive regarding this Pahawh Hmong written language and it has been largely ignored by scholars due to the account of its super-natural origin. Recently, however there has been an effort to learn more about the language, as scholars have concluded that regardless of its purport-ed origins, it is a very complex and orderly writing system, complete with vowels, consonants, and tonal accents, together with a numbering system and rules of syntax. Since the death of the Pahawh Hmong scripts author in 1967, there have been changes made until now there are three versions—a religious version, a first standard version, and a final version." Scholars are now surveying known Hmong nationals by census questionnaires to find those who have heard of, or can read or write, this language.[11]

Those Hmong who are willing to comment upon the Fillmore petro-glyphs, and the message left there by those who identified themselves as Hmong, indicate that the petroglyphs speak of a record or something gold and ancient that is still buried, ascribing authorship of the glyphs to those whose ancestors left the area prior to a great flood, hoping to return.

The Chalk Creek Petroglyphs

Cedar City was only a settlement on the Utah frontier when two men came to make their mark in history. Fred and George Ashdown were lum-bermen and thought that this would be a fine location for a new sawmill. They went into the canyons east of town to find a creek that would support their operation, and to locate a level place to build their sawmill. Near the head of Coal Canyon, just east and north of the new settlement, they dis-covered an old tunnel which had caved in. Curiosity got the best of the brothers so they decided to excavate the old mine because they belived it to be an old Spanish mine. They dug into the old tunnel for a distance of 200 feet or more. In the process, they discovered many interesting curios, including what they thought to be old iron tools that disintegrated when they picked them up. Several brass implements were also discovered and were shown around the settlement to those who were interested.

The brothers were unable to locate a suitable site for their sawmill in the area so they moved on to another town in the hopes of finding a site. Before they left, they gave a piece of ore that they had found to a friend, Ben Evans, who had the sample tested. He was surprised to learn that the sample was pure horn silver. Unable to locate the Ashdowns, he went into the canyon looking for the old mine without the benefit of a map or directions. He didn't spend a great deal of time in his search because of pressing matters at home. He gave up the search and never returned.

During the early 1920s, an old Mexican came into town with an old faded map. He spent many days riding throughout the hills and mountains east of Cedar City. He soon gave up his search but had befriended a rancher whom he had taken into his confidence. He told him he was looking for certain landmarks that would eventually take him to an old mine or cave. Not being able to locate what he hoped to find, he too left the area.

LaVan Martineau had heard about the Mexican Indian who could read the strange writings in Fillmore. He knew of a rock east of Cedar City with writings similar to those of the Fillmore outcropping. Part Indian, knowledgeable in the sign language, fluent in Indian tongues, versed in cryptoanalysis methods, here was a man with the right tools and the right background to tell the story. Not his story, but early man's story. He arranged to show the Cedar City writings to Jose Davila.

Davila told Martineau that they were not quite the same because there was no signature like those at Fillmore. Suddenly Martineau called to Davila that he had found some more writings. "I returned to confront five additional characters, one of them very similar to the signature in Fillmore, with only a slight but significant variant," stated Davila. "Yes, I had missed them in the original search. In fact my hand had actually rested on them when I passed by the rock."

These markings could have been the landmark the Mexican had spent so many hours looking for. Davila took pictures of these writings and then began the arduous task of interpretation. He eventually made it back to Mexico where he was arrested for artifact smuggling and sent to prison. He was released in the 1980s and still lives in Mexico.

Davila wrote about his translations and his idea concerning the two sites. He is quoted as saying, "After a thorough consideration of the activities of Moroni, it would not be far fetched to estimate we are considering here the resting place of the twenty-four plates of Ether."

Davila left an analysis of Moroni's steps after Cumorah and his presence in Utah, near Manti. Davila reports that this analysis is proven and now fully revealed. He stated:

Wanting to write some more after Mormon's death, Moroni found himself cumbersomely loaded with these large size plates of Ether. No ore, no room on the plates and in danger of being discovered by the Lamanite war party that had killed his father. He could not smelt ore, so he had to find a special kind of sedimentary sheet gold in a drift or fissure. He finally came upon this particular kind of gold about 38 miles from Manti, Utah. He made numerous plates there and spent the next twenty years engaged in the most [ambitious] literary achievement the world will ever know. The translation of the 24 plates of Ether.

Heavenly Counsel instructed him to conceal the plates of Ether and cross the plains towards New York State, where he was to leave the abridgment of Mormon. From the text of the inscriptions Moroni left in Utah, it seems he carved them after hiding the 24 plates of Ether in the Mountain-mine where he had found the gold to make extra plates by simply hammering them out. That is all the characters of the instructions to enter the mountain and his signature of the RED HAND; BUT NOT THE BASEBALL-LIKE SIGN! I strongly feel this time was many centuries later. In 1829 AD to be exact! This time he returned to bury the abridgment of Mormon he received from Joseph Smith after the completion of the Translation of the Book of Mormon.

DAVILA'S TRANSLATION OF THE CHALK CREEK PANEL

Character #1   KHNT – means *In front of, before, etc.*
Khn.t – means *At the beginning, begin.*
Kha-en-ta – means *measure.*

Character #2   Sh – means *pool, estate, or field.*
Bw – means *Abode, or Place.*
Sthait – means *a land measure equal to 52.300mts on each side, or 171' 8" for an area of 2/3 of an acre.*

Character #3   H aa, Hay – means *to go down, or descend.*

Character #4   A IMY – means *that which is in, or who is in.*

Character #5   TS.T, TCHU – means *Mountain*
BYA – means *Mine.*

Character #6   W P RNP. T – means *Festival of the new year, or the sun in the center of the skies and the four cardinal points.*

Character #7   DI – means *give.*
SBA – means *Door or gateway (Entrance) determinative use.*

Character #8 & #9 *S thait* – means *the land measure of 2/3 acres of land of*

 (reads as one)*171"8" on each side.*

Character #10   SA. T – means *Daughter.*

SBA – means *Star.*

 Khapesh – means *Constellation of the great Bear.*

Character #11   STHAIT – means *Land measure of 2/3 acres sq. of 171 '8"*
per side.

Character #12   YDB SAH YDB – means *Land betwen two river banks.*

Character #13   RDI – means *give, place or put.*

Character #14   Shwy – means *two.*

Character #15   SATU N SATU – means *Converging grounds or areas.*

Character #16   STHATT – means *Land measure of 2/3 acres sq. of 171' 8"*
per side.

Character #17   KHNT – means *In front of, or before.*

KHN . T – means *At the beginning, begin.*

 KHA * EN * TA – means *Measure.*

Character #18   SHA . T – means *One hundred cubits or 171' 8" ft".*

HA – means *at the back, retreat, descend.*

Qab – means *The middle of anything.*

Character #19   TEP – means *head, top, summit.*

Character #20   DR – means *remove.*

DAP – means *shelter or place of concealment.*

Character #21   DJB.T – means *brick, bar or ingot.*

YBHTY – means *precious stone.*

an – means *metal tablets upon which important texts have been recorded.*

The skull-like character at the head of the inscription means "Entrance to the Royal Crown Mountain."

Davila's translation of the ancient writings when put into text form would appear to read like the following:

Begin to measure an area of 2/3 acres sq. of 171' 8" per side at the beginning of the field which is in front of the mountain's descent. From the place where the mountain descends towards the north star, the daughter of the Great Bear Constellation measure 171' 8" and the sun in the Center of the Skies and the Four cardinal points, will hit upon the entrance of the mine at the converging area in the land between the two river banks putting a second measurement of 171' 8" ft. after beginning to measure one hundred cubits or 171' 8" from the back of the middle of the summit retreating to converge with the first measurement, to uncover or remove from their place of concealment precious ore, ingots and metal tablets upon which important texts have been recorded.

Using this method of translation, and if Davila is correct, it should be rather easy to figure out what the other 18 panels are saying. Davila went on to translate two more important characters.

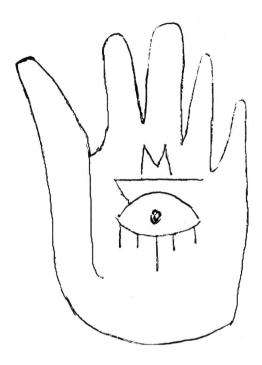

The Hand. It is a well-known symbol in Ancient America of the powerful hands of ITZAMNA. It is known as KABUL-ITZAMNA, the emblem of the Priesthood among the Mayas.

The "M" sign is a title in Egyptian. It is always used before a God, or important personage. Like M-Osiris, M-Seker, etc. It also means to "See." The "PLOUGH" which is the sign on top of the eye-like sign has a phonetical value of *mr*. MR–means "Love."

The "Eye" sign spells "NAI," literally, and means "Benevolent." The "Eyelashes and Eyelid" mean "Brilliance or beings of light." MORONAI, as priest-seer, loving and benevolent man of light.

The character like a baseball is formed by:
Pestch/Pauti + Thu/sper + Sa + Kd + is + Pestchie.
PESTCH PAUTI * THU*SPER * SA * KD * IS * PESTCHIU.
     1   2   3   4   5   6
"A man that was changed quickly into a luminous son of the three gods of heaven and earth and the underworld or the land of the dead."

1. Pestch or Pauti - *To Illumninate/shine or a very ancient God.*
2. Thu or Sper - *To come*
3. *SA* means *Man, Person or son.*
4. KD - *Character, go round, mould, form.*
5. IS - *To make haste.*
6. Pestchiu - *The three great gods of heaven and earth and the under world, or the land of the dead.*

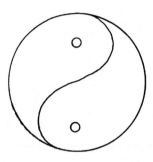

The above character stands alone above the three lines of the Chalk Creek Canyon panel. It appears to be the preface of the texts given in the following three lines. A close study of it will reveal twelve character combinations:

1. OAN - EARTH. Character Num. 26 of Joseph Smith's Egyptian Alphabet Sign List correlated by Jose O. Davila.

2. U-O-I Signs Z7 pg. 537 of *Gardiner's Egyptian Grammar.* Sign M17 Pg. 545 idem.

3. I or Y Sign Z4 pg. 537 interchangeable with the flowering reeds. *Gardiner's Egyptian Grammar.*

4. UANI, GARLAND OR CROWN. Pg. 146 B12 of *Budge's Dictionary.*

5. N, (Ripple of water) Sign N35 Pg. 490 of *Gardiner's Egyptian Grammar*, a preposition.

6. UANEN, THAT WHICH IS. Pg. 146 B13 of *Budge's Dictionary.*

7. Well Full of Water. Pg. 492. Sign 41-42 of *Gardiner's Egyptian Grammar.* This character has two Phonetics: HMT : MINERAL. Pg. 483 B9, *Budge's Dictionary.* Baa : "To work a mine or to dig out ore." Pg. 209 B last word, *Budge's Dictionary.*

8. The Jaw. Pg. 129 B 12, *Budge's Dictionary.* Part IV Pg. CVI Sign 33 of *Budge's Dictionary.* Has three Phonetics: <u>Ar-t</u> : Document. Pg. 129, A9, *Budge's Dictionary.* ART - Chamber. Pg. 130, A10, *Budge's Dictionary.* Aar-t - A Natural Block of Stone or a Kind of Stone. Pg. 112, A8 of *Budge's Dictionary.*

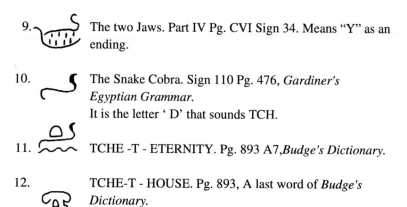

9. The two Jaws. Part IV Pg. CVI Sign 34. Means "Y" as an ending.

10. The Snake Cobra. Sign 110 Pg. 476, *Gardiner's Egyptian Grammar.*
It is the letter ' D' that sounds TCH.

11. TCHE -T - ETERNITY. Pg. 893 A7,*Budge's Dictionary.*

12. TCHE-T - HOUSE. Pg. 893, A last word of *Budge's Dictionary.*

These twelve signs and sign combinations are a system of Biliteral Sensegraphs used by the Priest of Ancient Egypt at the time of Abraham. It is a very concentrated form of writing as the reader can see. The phonetics in Egyptian of this preface character would be translated into English Syntax as follows: (Not the Egyptian Syntax)

E- (Ripple of Water) Letter ' N' which is a preposition: to.

Ga- (Well Full of Water) Baa - ' To dig out.'

E- Letter ' N' -preposition: of.

A- OAN - Earth (The span).

D- UANI - ' Garlanded.'

K- TCHE-T : ' Eternal.'

G- HEMT - ' Mineral.'

I- AR - T.I * ' Documents.'

F- UANEN - ' Which Are.'

L- 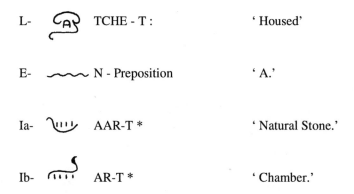 TCHE - T :   ' Housed'

E- 〰〰 N - Preposition   ' A.'

Ia- 〰 AAR-T *   ' Natural Stone.'

Ib- 〰 AR-T *   ' Chamber.'

The Preface to the text in the following three lines of Biliteral Sensesigns is translated: "TO DIG OUT OF EARTH GARLANDED ETERNAL MINERAL RECORDS WHICH ARE HOUSED IN A NATURAL STONE CHAMBER."

Following the rule stated as number 30 in *Gardiner's Egyptian Grammar*, pg. 36, that says: "The student must realize from the start that Egyptian is very sparing in its use of words meaning–"when, if, though, for, and, etc." Consequently, it often devolves upon the translation to supply the implicit logical "NEXUS" between sentences, as, "ALSO BETWEEN WORDS."

Similarly, distinctions of "TENSE" (of verbs) and "MOOD" (also) are not marked in the same way as in English.

Sign #2.

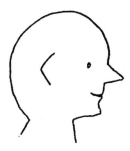

This character appears listed twice by Rodger Lambert's *Lexique Hieroglyphique*, Paris 1925. On Page 2B column, last two glyphs, reading as KHN-T or FND. On pg. 152, first word, Lambert translates this sign as: "LE COMMENCEMENT."

SIGN #3.

Rodger Lambert depicts this character identically on page 363 in the center of the middle column. Lambert also gives the hieroglyphic writing for this character in the next column as:

SIGN #4.

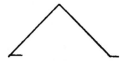

The walking legs are a very common sense sign in Egyptian. They generally accompany phoneograms spelling mothing, like: Go, come, enter, depart, stop, travel, etc. *Gardiner's Egyptian Grammar*, pg 457, lists this character as sign D54/55 giving one of its readings as SIDI:

SIGN #5.

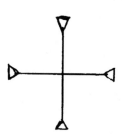

Gardiner's Egyptian Grammar, pg. 539, lists this character as sign Z11, called the "Crossed Planks." He says that in the Old Kingdom this sign began to replace sign M42, which is the "Flower Sign." He states this sign reads "IMY," which means "Who is in."

SIGN #6.

W. Erichsen Heft Schriftagfel, of Demotische Lesestucke, Leipsig 1937, lists this character, on page 11, as having several phonetics. On the seventh phonetic, he lists it reading "SH," and on the tenth phonetic as,

"TR." The sixth phonetics is letter "M," (the hieroglyphic OWL). We must consider the selection of these phonetics as influenced by the context. *Budge's Dictionary*, page 722, B6 and B14, says: "B6, SHA/SHAI, means, 'To fix, to appoint or to determine, etc.' B14, Shaa, means "Book, Writing or Document." On page 840, A10, *Budge's Dictionary*, says: "TER" means, "To Guide."

Consider the use of these last characters, 4, 5 and 6, as another proof of GENUINE EGYPTIAN WRITING of these petroglyphs. They read literally: "Go (From)—Who is in, Appointed, Writing, To Guide." This syntax is classic as an example of Egyptian verbal sentences with adverbial predicates. This word arrangement includes also the "Permission." Egyptian writings vest upon the translator, "To supply implicit logical NEXUS between sentences and also between words." Gardiner's *Egyptain Grammer* explains these rules in his lesson 11, pages 34, 35, and 36 listed as rules 27 to 30.

In Egyptian verbal sentences, the word order is: 1-Verb, 2-Subject, 3-Object, 4-Adverb or adverbial phrase. In this case, sign 4, the traveling legs are the verb: "Go, Travel, Departing, etc." Then follows the NEXUS "COPULA" of sign 5, the flower or crossed planks meaning: "Who is in," or "Who are to." Last is sign 6, ⌒⌒\ , which is used as the object: "Writing." The phonetical variants of this character, meaning "Appointed to guide" are intimately connected with the copula "Who are," of sign 5, as its adverbial predicate. There seems to be reason enough for this thought, for sign 6, ⌒⌒\ , secures also the value of the letter "M," typical of Egyptian writing of "Sentences with the "M," of Predication," explained as rule 38, page 40 lesson 111, of Gardiner's *Egyptian Grammar*. Letter "M" becomes the NEXUS "AS" in the context: "Travel - from Writings - Which are - Appointed - as - Guides." Therefore the complete translation of the first six characters could best be read in English Syntax as follows: "Begin a Sthait (an area of 100 cubits per side) departing from the inscriptions which are appointed as guides."

To carry out these instructions we must remember that the inscriptions face west at Chalk Creek. Therefore we must start at one side of the square going 100 cubits west from the petroglyphs. The question now, is, how far is one hundred cubits? Gardiner's *Egyptian Grammar* states on page 199, the "Meh" is a cubit measuring 20.6 inches or 523 millimeters. However, on page 48 of the book *Tutankhamen*, by Christiane Desroches-Noblecourt, published by Doubleday & Co. Inc., Garden City, New York, 1965, it is stated in the middle of the second paragraph, that in King Tut's tomb, four examples of the famous Egyptian unit of length were found. They measured one foot and seven and one half inches. *Budge's Dictionary* says on page 316 A8, that a cubit is 0.525 meters. Thus, one hundred cubits would be between 162.5 feet and 171'8." It is an important difference to consider with location and orientation of excavations.

According to Webster a "cubit" is a measure of length, originally the length of the forearm, from the elbow to the end of the middle finger: 18 inches or 45.72 centimeters. What was the value of the cubit length among these Egyptian writing cultures in America? No one seems to know. However, we can ascertain that the cubit is an ancient measure that varied from 18 to 21.5 inches, according to the race that ruled Egypt at different periods of time.

When Davila carried out the instructions at Fillmore, Utah, he found the measurement of the author of the petroglyphs. As he measured one side of the Sthait, he noticed a rock with a drill on top and an incision on the side exactly 85' 10" from the inscriptions. This is exactly half of a sthait 171' 8" long. On the other side of the sthait he found exactly 85' 10" from the southwest corner, or halfway up the side on the west of the square area, a stone carved hand. These two signs found at the middle of the sthait on an east-west axis were a sure indication to Davila that the ancient Egyptian writing cultures of America gave the cubit a value of 20.5 inches—171' 8" to a 100 cubits. Having thus accurately measured 171' 8" each 100 cubits going west from the Pertoglyphs, Davila resumed his translations.

SIGN #7.

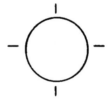

This is a compound ideogram. It depicts the "SUN" framed in the four cardinal points in the center of the firmament. The sun in this role becomes, "He who sits at the head of the four cardinal points or Knenti - Hensekt - t." On page 556, a last word of *Budge's Dictionary*, this ideogram has three components. 1). "The four Stokes," depicting "Hensekt-t," the "Four cardinal points." 2). "The circle that depicts the Periphery of the Firmament." 3). "The pellet in the center of the periphery depicting the Sun." Sir Allan Gardiner stated on page 539 and 490 of Gardiner's *Egyptian Grammar*, that the "Pellet" are signs Z8 and N33. It spells "Qedi" and means: "To mold, to form, etc. *Budge's Dictionary*, page 779, B6, says "Qet" means: "Design or plan." Budge says on page 743, B2, that the circle reads "Shenu" and means

"Periphery." This character then translates as: "Qeti-Shenu-Hensekt-t," which means: "Form the periphery (of the Sthait) within the four cardinal points."

Sign #8.

    This is another combination of determinative sensegraphs. The sign is formed by three characters. The glyph itself looks like a house. However, the roof is the conical loaf of bread that Gardiner's *Dictionary* identifies as sign X8 on page 533, and says that it means "Di," "give or place." Confirm page 622 A8, of Gardiner's *Egyptian Grammar*. In the middle kingdom, this conical sign was often replaced by the arm with a conical loaf on the hand, which is sign D37, page 454 of Gardiner's *Egyptian Grammar*. The bottom part of this glyph shows a door and the frame of a house. The frame of the house is the letter "P" and the entrance is the letter "T" or the cake of bread, sign Xl, page 531 of the same book. Now we have the root-word formed:

    D-P-T. *Budge's Dictionary* shows on page 877, B3, the word "TEPH–T." In Egyptian, the letter "T" is commonly written as a "D." Also, the "H" with the dot underneath is the silent emphatic, "H." Thus "TEPH-T" means: "cave, cavern or hole in the ground."

    Budge gives the hieroglyphic writing of "Hole in the Ground" as: which seems to have all the components of the present character, #8.

    Davila interpreted this glyph as reading "Udi-Teph-t," which means "Put Hole on the Ground." The idea given in characters #7 and #8, is: "Form the perimeter (of the Sthait) to the four cardinal points and put hole on the ground in the center of the perimeter."

Sign #9

    This character seems to be explained on page 200, rule 266, of Gardiner's *Egyptian Grammar* as a measure of land written in hieroglyphic as Gardiner says on page 521, sign V2, this is the written form or component phonetics of the STA, or Sthait, the Egyptian land measure. So the coil of rope was carved in the Chalk Creek Canyon texts of Central Utah in between the two circles that stand for the letter "T," which is the cupcake sign of Gardiner's sthait. *Budge's Dictionary* says that, "Sta-t" is a measure of land, that is 100 cubits per side. One must consider this Sthait variant to illustrate only the side of the sthait 100 cubits long and not the whole square area.

SIGN #10.

This is a well-known Egyptian character. It is the sign that determinates "Quality." Gardiner's *Egyptian Grammar* lists it as sign Z4, page 536. It illustrates the hieroglyphic pair of flowering reeds. This sign reads "Double" or "TY" as numeral "TWO." This is explained in lesson V1, page 58, rules 72 and 73 of Gardiner's *Egyptian Grammar*. One must consider this character as Numeral "2," besides its ideographic meaning of sides.

SIGNS #11 AND #12

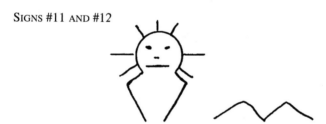

These two signs depict together the idea of embracing. The embracing arms, ⟨ ⟩of sign #11 are listed as sign D32, page 453, of Gardiner's *Egyptian Grammar*. It is a determinative sign meaning: *"Envelope or embrace."* The shining doll of sign 11 is a female and it could be read as "SA-T," page 610, of Gardiner's *Egyptian Grammar* and also page 584, A2, of *Budge's Dictionary*. Sign #12 is listed as a determinative sign on part VI, glyph 48, page CXIII, of *Budge's Dictionary,* and it means: "Constellation Meskhet—The Great Bear." To secure identification we should refer to page 544 of *Budge's Dictionary* listing it as "KHEPESH," meaning "The Constellation of the Great Bear." Thus, these two signs, according to the research done would mean: "Embracing the daughter of the constellation of the great bear" or the "North Star!"

SIGN #13.

The same as Sign #3, meaning a complete sthait of 100 cubits per side. We could read signs 9, 10, 11, 12 and 13 as follows: "STA-T SAT *KGEPESH - STHAIT," meaning: "Measure two sides 100 cubits long embracing the north star to complete the Sthait square area."

It is important to look at what Davila secured thus far, and to understand the readings and translations obtained. According to Davila's findings, he has translated Sign #1 to read: "To dig out of the earth, garlanded-everlasting-mineral records, which are housed in a natural stone chamber." Signs #2 through #6 commence a complete sthait (square area 100 cubits or 171' 8" perside) departing from the inscriptions which are appointed as "guides." Signs #7 and #8 form the perimeter of the sthait set with the four cardinal points and put "Hole on the ground in the center of the periphery."

Signs #9 through #13 measure two sides 100 cubits embracing the North Star, or the daughter of the constellation of the Great Bear to complete the Sthait area.

SIGN #14

This is a very interesting ideograph. It has no equal in Egyptian dictionaries. However, it is possible to discern three distinctive glyphs. The ' X' or cross sign is identified on page 538, sign Z9 of Gardiner's *Egyptian Grammar* as the determinative sign of actions involving something crossed or encountered. This crossing sign shows a "l" stroke underneath the intersection point. This stroke is sign Z1, page 534 of Gardiner's *Egyptian Grammar*. The stroke under an ideogram depicts exactly what the ideogram denotes—in this case, the intersection point, which is a very important location, for we are told we are to put a "hole on the ground" in the center of the sthait. The third glyph is a repetition of sign #10, meaning "two sides." This means we are to put an encountering cross departing from the ends of the last two sides we measured on the sthait. This sign reads: "WA. Dai-Ty."

SIGN #15

    This sign is the hieroglyphic form of sign D46, page 455 of Gardiner's *Egyptian Grammar*. It is the Phonetical "D." We have learned this sign interchanges or is replaced by the conical loaf of bread, and means "Put, Place, and reads." This sign is a reoccurrence of glyph #10 and it has been deciphered as meaning "Two."

SIGN #16

    This sign is a recurrance of glyph #10 and it has been deciphered as meaning, "Two."

SIGN #17

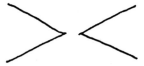

    This is truly an elucidating ideogram carrying the idea of the encountering cross sign of glyph #14. It is formed by encountering ideograms listed as sign M44 page 484 of Gardiner's *Egyptian Grammar* which serves as a determinative sign in related words with the letters "SPD" or "SHPD." (Author's note: Found on page 597, B6, of *Budge's Dictionary*, the word "S-pet," meaning "to make, to stretch or to make to extend; or cause to stretch or extend." The message conveyed in this ideogram is "to extend two converging lines and cause them to cross.")

SIGN #18

It has been shown that this sign means the complete sthait or an Egyptian land measure of 100 cubits per side, and it is the third time it appears on these inscriptions. Consider characters 14, 15, 16, 17 and 18. Here is a beautiful example of an Egyptian verbal sentence again–this time with the "sedjemef" verb form with the verb RDI that means "Give-put-place or cause" in a typical verbal sentence with a noun clause.

The typical verbal sentence construction is: I-Verb, II- Subject, III-Object, IV-Adverb or adverbial phrase, V-The Noun Clause used here. One of the meanings of sign #14 is the "two lines that cross or encounter," which is the subject. The other component meaning of sign 1 is the stroke under the intersection point which marks the object depicted or sought, and the adverbial phrase uses the adverb of place, "upon" the land bordered by the two sides of the sthait last measured, with the last component meaning of sign #14.

Gardiner shows as rule 69 on page 56 of lesson V that it is "a striking characteristic of Egyptian," the ease with which it can treat an entire sentence as a NOUN. In this case the complete sign #14, ⋈, is used as a "subject" of its passive, using the ensuing characters in a "passive" adverbial sentence, to be used complete as a noun clause of sign #14.

To determine this, we study the next sign #15, 𓂋, and its determined meaning—"put-give or place." This sign is used here as the verb of a new verbal sentence. The subject is to follow next in sign #16 which is the two lines whose "object" is to "extend," shown in sign #17, across the noun, sign #18, the sthait. Thus sign #17, ⟩⟨, S-pet, in its sedjemef form, is used here as the subject of the preceding verb in sign #15, RDI, meaning—"put-give, place." Because sign #15, the verb RDI, uses the following signs #16, 17 and 18 as a "noun clause," its meaning changes to "cause or allow"—rule 70 page 56, lesson V, of Gardiner's *Egyptian Grammar*. This second verbal sentence begins with sign #15 and uses signs 16, 17 and 18 as its noun clause. Signs 15, 16, 17 and 18 now read: "Allow two lines to converge and cause them to cross the Sthait." This becomes that adverbial passive subject of ideogram #14, ⋈, and is also used here as a complete new noun clause. Because "after" (you) allow two lines to converge and cause them to cross the sthait, only then can you determine the intersection point of these crossing lines which is marked by the stroke under glyph #14—upon which we are to put "a hole on the ground," described in signs #7 and #8.

SIGN # 19

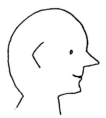

This sign is another repetition. It first appears as sign #2. It means "KHENT, commence."

SIGN #20

This character looks like a pair of ram's horns. It is formed by three glyphs, according to the research done. The upper part is listed as a complementary sign or determinative of "one hundred." That is the only value given to it by Gardiner's *Egyptian Grammar* on page 191 and 192 lesson XX. It is called "Shat," rule 259 and 260. (Author's note: This character is what made Davila excavate all over the mountain and drill 641 feet of exploratory holes trying to intercept the cavern described in sign #1. It was not until he ordered on credit a set of $45.00 *Budge's Dictionaries* that he learned that this upper "coil of rope sign" has the value of 40 cubits and is used as a determinative sign that accompanies Khet-en-Nuh, page 567, A7 of *Budge's Dictionary* meaning 40 cubits or 21.31 mts. *Budge's Dictionary* explains on page 567, A6, that this coil-of-rope sign is a land measure of 40 and of 100 cubits. Therefore, like Sir Allan Gardiner says on rule 266 of his *Egyptian Grammar*, the square sthait is also called the Khet. For this particular reason Davila spent $4,123.00 exploring and drilling 60 cubits beyond the true measurement.)

The connecting middle glyph is listed by W. Erichsen's Demotische Lesestucke, 3 heft sherifttafel alphabet, as illustrating the "H" or "H." *Budge's Dictionary* page 457, B Last, says "Ha" means "The back of the head." Page 457, A4, says it also means "To retreat." Page 439, A7, says "Ha" means "To descent, to go down, to enter." The bottom glyph is listed on page 466, sign F46, of Gardiner's *Egyptian Grammar* and reads "Qab," meaning: "Intestines." *Budge's Dictionary* page, 763, A6 and 7, says "Qab" means "Intestines or the middle of anything." Thus the complete reading and translation of Sign #20 would be: "Khet-en-Nuh. Ha. Qab, 40 cubits descending into the intestines or inside."

SIGN #21

This sign is listed on page 449 as sign D1 in Gardiner's *Egyptian Grammar*. It means "Top of Head." *Budges' Dictionary* says that it means "High Ground." Page 457, B last, shows this sign D1 as the determinative of "Ha" that means "The back of the head." Davila was quoted as saying at this point: "Thus we feel secure on the measurements being done on the west of the Ridge, that would be the back of the "High Ground" or "Summit"—the front being the eastern side of the ridge.

We are to begin or commence a hole in the ground 40 cubits or 21.31 mts (68'4") descending inside the back of the summit, at the center of the sthait, carefully measured before. At the present time, we are over 20 feet deep at this intersection point on the center of the sthait.

SIGN #22

This sign is formed by the hand that reads "DR" or "TER," meaning "To drive out." Page 884, A10, of *Budge's Dictionary*. Gardiner's *Egyptian Grammar*, page 602, B19, says "DR" or "TER" means "To Remove." The hand shows two glyphs in the wrist. On page 786 B8 of *Budge's Dictionary,* we find the hand with the two squares, meaning "Place of Concealment or Shelter;" "KAP." Thus the translation of sign #22 would be: "DR-KAP—Remove from place of Concealment."

Sign #23

This character finishes the three lines of inscriptions of the west-facing rock in Chalk Creek Canyon. Roger Lambert's Lexique *Hieroglyphque* shows this identical character on page 38, C5, meaning "an or en" and "metal tablets with important text engraved." In Davila's notes he said: "The translation of signs 19, 20, 21, 22 and 23 tell us: Commence descending 40 cubits (68' 4" or 21.31 meters) into the insides of the back of the summit, to remove from place of concealment, metal tablets upon which important texts have been engraven!"

The most important of all the characters is the "Signature" or "KEY" symbol, found not only in Chalk Creek, but in eastern Utah where four lead tablets were found. They will be discussed in the following chapter.

Next to the inscriptions, on a separate rock facing north, appears a set of two characters, Signs #24 and #25.

Sign #24

This is a compound-sense sign. It does not appear in such a form in any Egyptian dictionary. However, it is possible to discern several Egyptian characters in this "Baseball" -looking sign.

1. The circle. Page 910, A5, of *Budge's Dictionary* identifies the circle as "TCHERTCHER." Page 908, B last, says "TCHER" means "All the Whole." Page 909, kB5, says "TCHER" means "To construct."

2. The divided circle. Listed as page 486, sign N9 of *Gardiner's Egyptian Grammar*. It is a phonetical determinative of "Pestch—to shine."

3. The inverted "S." Shown on page 34, sign JJ2, of W. Erichsen's *3 Heft Schrifttafel of Demitische Lesestucke*. It shows the upper part of the inverted "S" to be the dipthong, "AI" and the lower part of the inverted "S" to be letter "U." Thus the phonetic reading "iu" is formed. Page 30, A12, of *Budge's Dictionary* says "Aiu" means: "Change or Transformation."

4. The inverted "S" inside the circle. This glyph now reads "PESTCH.IU." Page 250, B last, of *Budge's Dictionary* says that the meaning is "The three Great Gods of Heaven, and of Earth, and of the Spirit World" (the Tuat)…" etc.

5. The pellet. Already previously identified as a component sign of character #7, it is listed on page 538 as sign Z8 or M33 of Gardiner's *Egyptian Grammar*, meaning "To form or to mold" (Qoti).

6. The circle with the lower pellet. It is phonetical "pat" or "Pat," page 532, sign N6 of Gardiner's *Egyptian Grammar*. *Budge's Dictionary* says "Pat" means "He who." See page 233, B7.

7. At this point it is a good idea to introduce another phonetic value of the inverted "S" inside the circle before considering it as a component glyph of another sign. Page 30, B12, of *Budge's Dictionary* says "nu" means "to be."

8. The circle with the inverted "S" and the lower pellet. It reads "Pau-t," meaning: "Matter or Substance," Page 230 B5 of *Budge's Dictionary*.

9. The inverted "S" forms a comma inside the circle. Page 467, sign F51, of Gardiner's *Egyptian Grammar* says that this comma was used as an adaptation in Hieratic for "Son." Page 474, Sign H8, of Gardiner's *Egyptian Grammar* confirms the translation of "Son."

10. The inverted "S" also forms a reversed comma inside the circle. Gardiner says on page 467, sign F51, footnote #4 that this sign also spells "IS" and *Budge's Dictionary*, Page 143 B9, says "IS" means "To Make Haste."

This compound character could be read and translated into English as:

6.	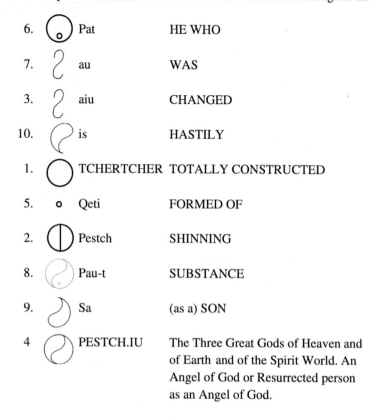 Pat	HE WHO	
7.	au	WAS	
3.	aiu	CHANGED	
10.	is	HASTILY	
1.	TCHERTCHER	TOTALLY CONSTRUCTED	
5.	Qeti	FORMED OF	
2.	Pestch	SHINNING	
8.	Pau-t	SUBSTANCE	
9.	Sa	(as a) SON	
4	PESTCH.IU	The Three Great Gods of Heaven and of Earth and of the Spirit World. An Angel of God or Resurrected person as an Angel of God.	

SIGN #25.

This rather impressive character is not found anywhere on Egyptian texts. It is considered a personal name and is a complex form of:

SIGN #1   The red Ochre-painted hand put over the chiseled character. Page 455, Sign D46 of Gardiner's *Egyptian Grammar*
says "DRT" means "Hand." We have the impression that

this Red Hand is used here in a typically American cus-
tom, shown in the ruins of America or rather middle
America, which is acknowledged as the cradle of
American civilizations. In the ruins, we can find the
"RED HAND" imprint on walls and Korbell Arches. This
is recognized as the "Powerful hands of Kabul-Itzamna of
the Maya" or the "Powerful hands of Heaven." *Budge's
Dictionary,* page CVIII, part IV, signs 77 and 78 says that
"Hand" reads "TCHA-T." Also. page 895, B12, of
Budge's Dictionary says that "TCHA-T" means "Garment
or Apparel." This tends to give the red hand the meaning
of "Power to Wear as a Garment."

SIGN #2

The Crown-like sign. This is recognized as page 5, sign
V36, of Gardiner's *Egyptian Grammar.* It is the name of a
receptacle of some kind given to a temple. It is the phonetical determinative of "HEN." There is another identification
of this phonetical reading found on *Budge's Dictionary*
page,   CVIII glyph, 95 part IV, that gives this character
the reading of "HEN," meaning "Procreate." Page 486,
B10 of *Budge's Dictionary* says "HEN" means "To
Administer." Page 487 says "HENU" means
"Possessions." The "U" ending is secured by the hook bar
under the crown, which is the letter "U." The meaning of
these two component glyphs of character #25, the RED
HAND and the hook-based crown, would be "Minister and
possessor of the power garments" or simply "Minister and
owner or bearer of the Priesthood." (Author's Note: It is
with difficulty that this conclusion of Davila's is accepted.
It should be noted that not all of the translation came directly from Budge and Gardiner. Some of Davila's translations
came directly from himself, by way of the supernatural.)

SIGN #3

This sign is the Plow or Hoe listed on page CXXXIX,
character #14 of part XX in Budge's *Dictionary of determinative Bilateral Signs.* It spells "MR" and means
"Love." This identity is further secured on page 516, sign
U6 of Gardiner's *Egyptian Grammar.* It is phonetical
"MR" and sometimes is used in place of sign U8, ‹,
with a phonetical value of "HN."

SIGN #4

This component sign is the complementary bilateral deter-minative listed on page 346, B9, of *Budge's Dictionary,* reading "N A I." It means "Good" or "Benevolent." (Here Davila explains that he feels the reading of the component signs #3 and #4 would be: "MORONAI" meaning "Goodness and Benevolence Lover."

SIGN #5.

This is the Sther-t sign for "Eyelash" or Sether-t for "eye-lashes," page 630, A14, of *Budge's Dictionary.* Hence this component sign has a phonetical value of "STHS." On page 630, A Last, *Budge's Dictionary,* we find a determinative sign, , that reads "S-THES," meaning "To Exalt." Again on page 630, A15, it shows the upper eyelash, reading "S-THEHEN," meaning: "To Scintillate."

SIGN #6.

This sign, formed by the upright hand and the eye inside, complete with the pupil, is found on page 865, B5, *Budge's Dictionary,* reading, "TA-ARI," and meaning "To cause to do, to make or be done."

SIGN #7.

This sign is formed by the hand and the pupiless eye inside. The absence of the eyeball in the eye renders the glyph as a possible "R" or "mouth," page 452, sign D21, Gardiner's *Egyptian Grammar.* The "R" sound seems to apply here. Budge's Dictionary shows it on page 884, B9, reading "TERU," which means "A light God called TUAT X."

This completes the last character of the Fillmore inscriptions. This last signature sign can be read: "MORONAI, Lover of goodness and benevolence. Minister and possessor of the Power Garments brilliantly exalted. A God of light."[12]

Jose O. Davila stated in November of 1965 that on these inscriptions, "Angel Moronai" gave instructions to "retrieve from place of concealment, metal tablets upon which important texts have been recorded." That state-ment, according to Davila, led him to try to identify which records Angel

Moronai had, "and which records did Moronai, the man-prophet, have. These two sets of records he concealed or hid in the backyard of the Mormon people in Utah." But when?

Davila concluded that as soon as he found a way to finance the re-excavation of the Fillmore mine he would retrieve the ancient records found there. However, Jose O. Davila will most likely never return to the site of the ancient writings. If there are records to be retrieved, it will be by someone who would be chosen to do so.

Ancient writings found above the town of Nephi, Utah.

FOOTNOTES

1. Budge, Sir Wallis, *Egyptain Language.*
2. Budge, Sir Wallis, *Egyptian Language.*
3. *Pearl of Great Price*, Church of Jesus Christ of Latter Day Saints.
4. Paper by Dr. Paul Cheesman.
5. Gardiner, Sir Allan. *Egyptian Grammar.*
6. Gardiner, Sir Allan. *Egyptian Grammar.*
7. Nibley, Dr. Hugh. *Professor, Brigham Young University.*
8. Court records from Millard County, Utah.
9. Interview in possession of the Author.
10. Interview in possession of the Author.
11. Cheesman, Dr. Paul R. and David L. Tomlinson. *Egyptian and Hmong clues to a Western American Petroglyph Group.*
12. Gardiner, Sir Allan. *Egyptian Grammar.*

CHAPTER 7
OTHER WRITINGS, ARTIFACTS AND CONCLUSIONS

As mentioned before, there are several sites that bear the symbols shown in the previous chapter. A study was first updated and published by Albert B. Elsasser and E. Contreras in California during the mid 1950s. It adds significant finds in Idaho and Utah, and additional sites in California and Nevada. In addition to the four categories of elements identified by Elsasser and Contreras, this study identifies a pervasive Egyptian influence.

Originally, seven sites were identified by Elsasser and Contrera which contained elements that were distinctive and not recognized in the more than 200 petroglyph sites recorded within the same general area. Four of the sites are within a 35-mile radius of Oakland, California. The other three sites are more widely located, within a 250 mile radius of Oakland: one north near Dunsmuir, California; one east, near Genoa, Nevada; and one southeast, near Lone Pine, California.[1]

The sites are by location and survey numbers:

1. Rockville, Solano County, CA, called "SOL-16."
2. Tilden Park, Alameda County, CA, called "TILDEN PARK #1, and "TILDENPARK #2."
3. Claremont Creek, Alameda County, CA, called "ALA-19."
4. Vargas Road, near Mission San Jose, Fremont, Alameda County, CA, called "ALA-51."
5. Castle Crags, near Dunsmuir, Shasta County, CA., no survey number given.
6. Shoshoni Cemetery, Alabama Hills, Inyo County, CA., no survey number given.
7. Genoa, Douglas County, NV, no survey number given.

Subsequently, the following seven sites have been identified as containing the same elements, sizing, composition etc., removed by up to 1000 miles from the original groups found:

8. Pocatello, ID, 12 glyphs.
9. Nephi, UT, 9 glyphs, 8 in one group, one removed about 75 feet.[2]

10. Manti, UT, 27 glyphs, 5 removed about 100 feet from the rest.
11. Fillmore, UT, 27 glyphs.
12. Cedar City, UT, 45 glyphs.
13. Lake Powell, San Jaun County, UT, 4 glyphs.[3]
14. Parrette Draw, Uintah County, UT, 25 glyphs.[4]

THE LEAD TABLETS OF THE DESERT

In a remote canyon south of Myton, Utah stands a cliff face with symbols that are believed to be of Spanish origin. In a previous publication, "Of Men and Gold," by this author, the symbols are interpreted as Spanish. At the bottom of the panel is a lone symbol that was not totally explainable until found again alone several miles away on a flat rock resting on a mound. Under the flat rock was another flat rock that not only bore the symbol but a host of others that are like those mentioned previously.

The author poses by the symbols in the remote canyon area of Pariette Draw.

The flat rock found in the mound.

In this mound were found several rusted pieces of metal that crumbled at the touch. It was not until several years later during an excavation of the mound that a small stone box was uncovered about 4 feet down. The box was nothing more than six flat stones placed together to form a box. Inside the box were four metal tablets. Three of the tablets were flattened while one was rolled up. It appeared that they were made of lead. The tablets were removed and further excavation was halted at the time. The tablets were taken to several authorities to have them examined, but they were dismissed as fakes. No further attempt to have them authenticated has been made at this time. The strange thing about these tablets are the writings themselves. As the reader will see, there are at least three different types of writing on these tablets. The one thing that stands out the most is the fact that one of these writings is like those found in the Soper/Savage collection. How did it get in that mound? The other tablets resemble a cuneiform type of writing. This is not very understandable.

The Lead Tablets of Pariette Draw

The following are close-ups of the tablets:

188

189

THE GIANT SUN OF DIAMOND FORK

This giant "Sun" symbol, found in a side canyon in Diamond Fork Canyon, Utah County, Utah, was hidden from public view for hundreds of years until recently. It has now been subject to destruction by Scout groups and others who have little or no respect for ancient writings or rock art. Using the compass and standing directly in front of the symbol, you face due east. The rays of the sun have a purpose, as does the hole at the left on the first ray. It is not a bullet hole, but a hole carved there by the artist. The symbol is cut into the rock ³/₈ of an inch deep and the circle is 30 inches across. Below the symbol is the old Spanish Trail. There are Spanish symbols found within close proximity of this sun symbol, but it's doubtful that they are interconnected in any way.[5]

During the early 1920s, a father and his two sons were hunting deer up in what is known as "Monk's Hollow," off Diamond Fork Canyon. It had been a mild fall and the three decided to hike into the red cliffs to see what they could find. The father got separated from his sons so he decided to head down to the road to wait for them. In the meantime, the two young men were hunting along the face of the cliffs when all of a sudden the weather changed for the worse, and a major snow storm came in. They were soon besieged by a harsh north wind and blinding snow. They inched their way along the cliff-face, feeling for a crevice they could slip into to wait out the storm. Soon they found what they had hoped to find, a small cave. They quickly slipped inside and sat down to wait out the blinding snow storm. The father had made his way to the car and sat there waiting for the storm to abate. Meanwhile the boys decided to see what was in the cave as far as tinder, so that they could light a fire to stay warm during their stay in the cave. They found tinder that had been brought in by pack rats, and in a short while they had a warm fire. Now that they had some warmth and a source of light, the two decided to explore the small cave to see what else was there. It was with great surprise that they found a small chest partially hidden in the back of the cave. It had two straps around it that buckled in the front and a large round lock held the lid secure. They tried to break the lock by hitting it with the butts of their rifles and with boulders but this proved to be futile. Then one of the brothers decided to shoot the lock off. With a blast from his 30-40 Krag the lock disintegrated. They lifted the lid and beheld a vast treasure of gold coins. They each dug into the chest and filled their pockets with the small golden coins and then covered the chest with rock and brush that was inside the cave. They could hardly contain themselves and talked of what great things this treasure could bring. Soon the snow stopped falling and the sun came out.

The boys made their way out of the cave and slowly moved down the mountain to where their father was waiting on the road. When the father heard their story and saw the gold coins with his own eyes, the threesome placed their rifles in the trunk of the car and began to hike back to the cave, following the boy's footprints in the snow. However, the hike back to the cave came to an abrupt halt. No sooner had the three climbed onto the rock ledges than the storm, once again, was upon them. The snow came at them in a blinding fury and it was all that they could do to get themselves off the mountain and back to their car. They barely made it out of the canyon at all. The winter winds and blowing snow kept the men out of the canyon all the rest of the season, but they had high hopes of retrieving the treasure as soon as the warm spring winds melted the snow in Diamond Fork Canyon.

When the snow was gone off the mountain the three men headed back up to see if they could get to the treasure chest. They talked of all that they were going to buy with their share of the gold while driving up the winding mountain road. Soon they came to the place that they had parked the car during the deer hunt. They got out of the car and started to hike up into the cliffs and to the treasure cave. Hours went by and no cave was found. They regrouped and tried again to find the cave. No luck. They could not find the cave. Nothing looked like it did the day that they found the cave. The landmarks were not the same; nothing was the same. They became angry, and they began to shout at each other, blaming one another for not remembering the landmarks and the trails. Soon they were so upset that they decided to go home and then try again the next day. Day after day went by, week to week, and month to month, and still no cave was found. They had wasted the whole summer looking for the cave and found nothing. Soon they decided to give it up and wait until the first snow fall to try again. The winter months that followed kept the men out of the mountains that year and soon their minds were dimmed as to the location of the cave at all. They gave up the search. The father died some years later, as did the older brother. The youngest brother kept seven coins until he, too, died. 6 This author has inspected the coins and could see that they are Spanish. Somewhere up Diamond Fork Canyon is the treasure of the sun. Will anyone ever find it again?

Diamond Fork Canyon and Monks Hollow.

An old Mexican coin found in the Narrows near the Sun symbol.

THE CURRANT CREEK COPPER BOWL

Just a few years ago a man was fishing on Currant Creek, Duchesne County, Utah, when he came upon a copper object in the sand, just out of the water of the creek. Bending over, he brushed the sand from the object. To his surprise he could see that it was a bowl of sorts. He dug the object out of the sand and then washed it off in the creek. There in his hand was a large copper bowl with a beautiful but strange design around the inside edge and a very strange inscription in the bottom of the bowl. He didn't know, nor did he fully understand, what he had found. He took it home and used it as his dogs water bowl for several weeks until he was told that what he had was very old, and most likely something that could be of Aztec origin.[7]

The copper bowl found on Currant Creek

The strange design in the bottom of the bowl. There are several other small markings on the bottom of the bowl as well.

The Currant Creek area holds many secrets. It is a well-known fact that the Spanish miners used this area for gold smelting, and it is a known fact that there are several old mines in the canyon. Did the miners have Aztec slaves? Or, were the old mines dug by the Aztecs themselves? Who were really the first in Currant Creek? We may never know!

This is an old Spanish mine in Currant Creek.

THE EGYPTIAN BELTS

There have been at least eight different belts of Egyptian design found in North America. How they got here is anyone's guess. Three young women were hiking just east of Provo, Utah, near what is known as Rock Canyon, when one of the young women found a copper or bronze triangle with Egyptian hieroglyphs on it. They took the piece to Brigham Young University and had several faculty members look at it. It was soon dismissed as a possible forgery.

A Mr. Jessee Roots of Salt Lake City, Utah discovered a belt in a field in Illinois, sometime prior to 1940. It was covered with hieroglyphics and had a triangle at one end similar to the Provo triangle, yet dissimilar enough that it was not an exact replica. It, too, was dismissed as a forgery.

A similar belt was discovered near Wellsville, York County, Pennsylvania, and reported by Dr. W. W. Strong of Mechanicsburg,

Pennsylvania, a physicist. It was very similar to the Illinois belt. Dr. Strong was one of the founders of the Phoenician Historical Society of America.

In 1934 near the Columbia river in Arlington, Oregon, Tom McMullen found a belt while excavating at a depth of four feet. It had two squares and triangles intact as well as five out of six connecting links.

In a cave in New Mexico, a wheeled toy was discovered that appeared to be of an ancient origin. Nearby a metal belt was found. It appeared to be a copper/zinc alloy, and all squares and triangles in addition to all six connecting links were intact. Some detached circular medallions were unearthed at the same site. The similarity to the Oregon belt is striking, but again sufficient difference exists to indicate that each belt is a unique, custom creation.

In Somerville, Alabama, a belt was found by a Negro farm hand by the name of Pete Draper near what was known as Lacey's Spring. He gave it to the present owner, a Mr. Wilhoite. The belt is still intact, with the curious substitution of an Indian with a tomahawk and feather headdress in place of an Egyptian figure on one of the circular medallions.

In a Kansas cow pasture, a belt was found, but had only the circular medallions on it. The figures engraved on them are strikingly similar to the figures found on the other belts.

In Newton, Illinois, a Mr. Larry Bigard found a medallion similar to the triangular pieces already disclosed.

In a phone interview December 8, 1993, with Dr. Hugh Nibley of Brigham Young University, he said that he and Joseph Ginart examined some of the belts that were found up and down the foothills throughout Utah and after much deliberation they concluded that the belts (in fact, all of the belts) are of recent and Masonic origin. [8]

However, a letter dated March 2, 1973 from Paul R. Cheesman sheds a different light on Nibley's findings. The letter is as follows:

March 2, 1973

Mr. and Mrs Richard Spivey
1966 N. Macdonald
Mesa, Arisona 85201

Dear Brother and Sister Spivey:

I have appreciated your sending me the photographs of the metal belt. We have concluded that this is definitely of Egyptian origin and had its influence on whoever and wherever it was made.

I would be interested in learning what the American Museum of Natural History had to say. I also am very interested in the wheeled toy you mentioned and would appreciate a photograph of that.

Sincerely, Paul Cheesman [9]

THE NEW MEXICO EGYPTIAN BELT

There are many more spectacular artifacts that have yet to be found. There are many that are in the clutches of unscrupulous men who, with a simple flip of their wrists, dismiss each and every claim as fraudulent and misleading. Yet they hold on to the artifacts with a death grip. There have been too many artifacts and old writings found to be fraudulent. Perhaps the greatest question is why none of these writings and artifacts have surfaced through normal archaeological digs? Why have tablets and plates of gold, lead and rock with inscriptions unceasingly come into light from the flashlight of the prospector looking for the gold, the farmer planting his field, the amateur adventurist hiking the hills, the uneducated school boy looking for bugs? We may never know the answer to these questions. As we look at the whole picture, we see that only the surface has been scratched, and that there are many more tombs to uncover, many more artifacts to find, and many old writings to decipher. We do not defend the ambitious acts of those who would adventure into the tombs of the past without knowledge and educational background on the subject, but then again, it is not cause to classify those finds as deceptive or fraudulent because of their lack of knowledge or experience. It is important to learn as much as possible so that when a find is made, all possible precautions are taken to assure its authenticity.

The following charts outline the different characters found on all of the different tablets, plates and artifacts mentioned in this book. It is exciting to see how many of these symbols occur with different artifacts and rock writings. Most of the writings are gone now, but there are still a few around. If you, the reader, happen upon symbols that are similar to the ones viewed in this book, it is imperative that you photograph them and log their exact location. Preserving the treasures of the ancients is a task that will be ours until we leave this mortal existence, and then the task will fall upon the shoulders of our children.

FOOTNOTES

1. Cheesman, Dr. Paul R., F.E.S. and David L. Tomilinson. A paper presented at the World Cultures of Ancient America Congress of the Epigraphic Society, June 5, 1988, held in San Francisco, California.
2. This second symbol found was the "Life" symbol like that of the Egyptians. Found by the author.
3. These 4 glyphs were found approximately 7 miles southeast of Lake Powell, Utah. Found by the author.
4. Found by the author.
5. Shown to the author by a friend.
6. Events revealed to the author by Louis Steadman on August 11, 1978.
7. Bowl was shown to the author by the finder, who wishes to remain anonymous.
8. From information obtained from the Records of Dr. Paul Cheesman. and from sources attending lectures by Dr. Cheesman.
9. Copy of letter in possession of author.

CHART OF CHARACTER COMPARISONS OF VARIOUS ANCIENT WRITINGS

Egyptian Heiratic J.S.Facsimiles Anthon Trans Padilla No.					Ecuador-Crespi Soper-Savage Kinderhook Manti W				Commentary
									No. system is digest of Padilla glyphs.
105	〗	〗	〗						
106	°〗		〗°			°〗	𝓎		
107	〗			J					
108	𝟤								
109	↺	⁓	𝓋		𝓋	〗	⊂		
110	⌐								
111	⇁								
112	↻								
113	⊢⁀								
114	⇀⁀					⌐		⌐°	
115	⊂°								
116	𝛾					𝛾	𝜈	⤢	
117	⋋	⋌							
118	⅄°		⅄						
119	⁰⊤		⁰π					⁰⊤	
120	⊥°	⊥	⊥°		⟍		⊥°		
121	⊥°								
122	+	+	+				+		
123	/	/	/		/	/	/	/	
124	−	−	−			−			
125	‖		‖			‖	‖	‖	
126	Ⅱ		Ⅱ	Ⅰ	Ⅱ	π		π	
127	//		//				ₒ\\		
128	°		°				‾°		
129	≐		=			=	=		
130	≡°		≡					≡°	

201

CHART OF CHARACTER COMPARISONS OF VARIOUS ANCIENT WRITINGS

Egyptian Heiratic J.S.Facsimiles Anthon Trans Padilla No.					Ecuador-Crespi Soper-Savage Kinderhook Manti W			Commentary
								No. system is digest of Padilla glyphs.
131	⊙⊙		⊙⊙			⊙	⊙⊙	
132								
133								
134								
135							≡	
136								
137								
138								
139								
140								
141								
142								
143								
144								
145								
146								
147								
148								
149								
150								
151								
152								
153								
154								
155								
156								

202

CHART OF CHARACTER COMPARISONS OF VARIOUS ANCIENT WRITINGS

Egyptian Heiratic J.S.Facsimiles Anthon Trans Padilla No.				Ecuador-Crespi Soper-Savage Kinderhook Manti W					Commentary — No. system is digest of Padilla glyphs.
157	⪦						ʃ		
158	Ŝ						S̀		ᴅꞌᴀᴅ
159	ᴕꞌ						ᔕ		
160	ᴕꞌ								
161	S	S	S		S	S			
162	Ꞩ		Ꞩ			S			
163	S₀				S.	S.	S	·S·	S:
164	ᔕ				ᄂ		ᔕ		
165	⑤								
166	Ƨ	Ʒ							
167	Ʒ	Ƨ	Ƨ				·S	?ₖ	
168	Z					⅄			
169	Ż		Ż						
170	Z̤		Z̄						
171	ʻℋ	ʻℋ							
172	ʻℋ		ℋ		ℋ			ℋ	
173	Ч		Ч		Ч	Ч	Ч		Ч
174	Чʻ								
175	Ꮜ	Ч	Ꮜ						
176	᣸					Ч‟	L	Ꮞ	
177	Ⱶ		⁖ꞌ						
178	ꓭ		ᴴ		ᴴ		ᴴ		
179	ᴨ		ᴨ						
180	Ƴ		Ƴ		λ		Ƴ	Ƴ	
181	Ʋ						У		
182	Ƴ								

203

CHART OF CHARACTER COMPARISONS OF VARIOUS ANCIENT WRITINGS

Egyptian Heiratic J.S.Facsimiles Anthon Trans Padilla No.				Ecuador-Crespi Soper-Savage Kinderhook		Manti W	Commentary — No. system is digest of Padilla glyphs.
183	[glyph]						
184	[glyph]						
185	[glyph]						
186	[glyph]						
187	[glyph]						
188	[glyph]	[glyph]			[glyph]		
189	[glyph]						
190	[glyph]						
191	[glyph]						
192	[glyph]	[glyph]	[glyph]		[glyph]		
193	[glyph]				[glyph]		
194	[glyph]						
195	[glyph]						
196	[glyph]						
197	[glyph]						
198	[glyph]						
199	[glyph]						
200	[glyph]						
201	[glyph]			[glyph]	[glyph]	[glyph]	
202	[glyph]						
203	[glyph]	[glyph]			[glyph]		
204	[glyph]						
205	[glyph]	[glyph]	[glyph]	[glyph]			
206	[glyph]						
207	[glyph]				[glyph]		
208	[glyph]	[glyph]	[glyph]				

CHART OF CHARACTER COMPARISONS OF VARIOUS ANCIENT WRITINGS

Egyptian Heiratic J.S. Facsimiles Anthon Trans Padilla No.				Ecuador-Crespi Soper-Savage Kinderhook Manti W				Commentary
								No. system is digest of Padilla glyphs.
209	[glyph]							
210	[glyph]		[glyph]	[glyph]	[glyph]			
211	[glyph]					[glyph]	[glyph]	
212	[glyph]	[glyph]						
213	[glyph]							
214	[glyph]		[glyph]		[glyph]			
215	[glyph]							
216	[glyph]							
217	[glyph]							
218	[glyph]							
219	[glyph]							
220	[glyph]							
221	[glyph]		[glyph]	[glyph]				
222	[glyph]							
223	[glyph]							
224	[glyph]		[glyph]					
225	[glyph]		[glyph]		[glyph]	[glyph]	[glyph]	
226	[glyph]					[glyph]		
227	[glyph]							
228	[glyph]		[glyph]					
229	[glyph]				[glyph]		[glyph]	
230	[glyph]							
231	[glyph]		[glyph]			[glyph]	[glyph]	
232	[glyph]							
233	[glyph]							
234	[glyph]							

CHART OF CHARACTER COMPARISONS OF VARIOUS ANCIENT WRITINGS

Egyptian Heiratic J.S.Facsimilies Anthon Trans Padilla No.				Ecuador-Crespi Soper-Savage Kinderhook Manti W				Commentary
								No. system is digest of Padilla glyphs.
235								
236								
237								
238								
239								
240								
241								
242								
243								
244								
245								
246								
247								
248								
249								
250								
251								
252								
253								
254								
255								
256								
257								
258								
259								
260								

OTHER BOOKS BY THE AUTHOR

La Mina del Yutas, The Lost Josephine Mine
Out of print, but can be found in most public libraries in special collections.

Of Men and Gold
In most book stores.

SELECTED BIBLIOGRAPHY

Ancient Writing on Metal Plates — Dr. Paul R. Cheesman
Handbook of Middle American Indian — Albert P. Taylor
America's Ancient Civilizations — Hyatt Verrill

Ancient Burials of Metallic Foundation Documents in Stone. University of Illinois Graduate School of Library and International Science, Number 157, 1982.

An Egyptian Hieroglyphic Reading Book for Beginners — E.A. Wallis Budge

DE RE METALLICA. — Georgius Agricola

The Phoenician Origin of Britons, Scots & Anglo-Saxons — L. A. Waddell
The Sumerians — C. Leonard Woolley
The Indo-Sumerian Seals Deciphered — L. A. Waddell
The Archaeology of North America — Dean R. Snow
Vanished Civilizations of the Ancient World — Edward Bacon
A Study of Writing — I .J. Gelb
The Michigan Relics — James E. Talmadge